THE
CLEVELAND
CAVALIERS

A HISTORY OF THE
WINE & GOLD

······································

VINCE McKEE

THE
History
PRESS

Published by The History Press
Charleston, SC 29403
www.historypress.net

Front cover, top left: *Courtesy Sam Bourquin.*
Front cover, top right: *Courtesy Sheryl Scanlon.*
Front cover, bottom right: *Courtesy Sheryl Scanlon.*
Front cover, left: *Courtesy Landov Media.*
Back cover, top left: *Courtesy Elsa Spineli-DeLuca.*
Back cover, top right: *Courtesy Kenny Roda.*
Back cover, bottom: *Courtesy Kenny Roda.*

All facts in the book were verified with www.basketball-reference.com and the players themselves.

First published 2014

Manufactured in the United States

ISBN 978.1.62619.680.3

Library of Congress Cataloging-in-Publication Data

McKee, Vince.
The Cleveland Cavaliers : a history of the wine & gold / Vince McKee.
pages cm
ISBN 978-1-62619-680-3 (paperback)
1. Cleveland Cavaliers (Basketball team)--History. I. Title.
GV885.52.C57M45 2014
796.323'640977132--dc23
2014027397

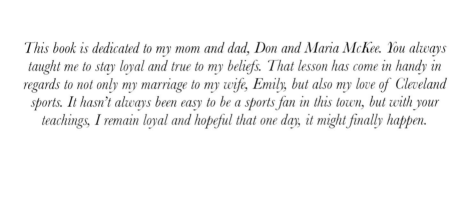

This book is dedicated to my mom and dad, Don and Maria McKee. You always taught me to stay loyal and true to my beliefs. That lesson has come in handy in regards to not only my marriage to my wife, Emily, but also my love of Cleveland sports. It hasn't always been easy to be a sports fan in this town, but with your teachings, I remain loyal and hopeful that one day, it might finally happen.

Contents

A Message to the Fans from Larry Nance and Craig Ehlo

I appreciated the fans when they cheered for us, and I still do now. They tell me how they loved our team because of how hard we played. I want the fans to know that when they see me, they are always welcome to come up and say hello. I will always stop for an autograph and shake a hand. I really appreciate our fans because we have the best fans in the world. I just want to say thank you!
—Larry Nance

I have a picture that hangs in my sports room that has Ozzie Newsome, Joe Carter and I, and we are all wearing each other's uniforms. I see that picture every day, and it just reminds of those seven years I was in Cleveland. The fans accepted you for who you were. They patted you on the back when you did good and picked you up when you were down. They wore their hearts on their sleeves and supported us no matter what. That is the biggest thing I can say to them—the camaraderie that we had with our team had a lot to do with those 20,000 people at the Richfield Coliseum every night. They supported you no matter what, and I have never come back to Cleveland and had anyone say anything negative to me. Every time I go back, fans tell me that they had a wonderful time watching our group play. I just want to thank them for supporting us for all those years. Even though we never won a championship, they loved us through and through.
—Craig Ehlo

Foreword

Find a comfortable chair and settle in, Cavaliers fans. Vince McKee is going to take you on a trip down memory lane in his new book, *The Cleveland Cavaliers: A History of the Wine & Gold*.

It's all there—from the early days at the Cleveland Arena to Ted Stepien and the Teddy Bears to the 2007 NBA Finals. McKee hasn't missed a thing. His thorough research and reporting is supplemented with lively interviews and anecdotes.

All your favorite old stories are included, but there are some new ones, too—like the one about Michael Jordan and Craig Ehlo and his son, Austin. After reading this, you won't be able to wait for the start of basketball season.

—*Mary Schmitt Boyer*

Foreword

If you bleed wine and gold like Mr. Cavalier—and I do—then this book is for you. Call it "Cavaliers from A to Z," or perhaps "Austin to Zydrunas."

The Cleveland Cavaliers: A History of the Wine & Gold takes you through the growing pains, when number thirty-four arrived, on through the Miracle of Richfield, when a Jim Chones broken foot stood between the Cavs and a ring. Read how World B. Free and George Karl kept basketball alive in northeast Ohio and how Wayne Embry assembled one of the best teams in the NBA during the late 1980s and early '90s.

The Mike Fratello days, prior to the unforgettable King James era, earned their own place in Cavs lore as the Cavs had arguably the best team in the land for back-to-back years, only to fall short in the post-season.

We all believe our Cavs passion will be rewarded someday, and so to you, loyal fans, enjoy this read as we salute a real wine-and-gold winner!

—Fred McLeod

Foreword

Ibleed wine and gold, and Cleveland is my home! The city is flourishing now and ready to accept a winner. I'm glad a book is being written so more people can hear about the team's rich history. We have come so close many times, and I believe that one day we can get over the hump!

—*Austin Carr*

Acknowledgements

This book would have not been possible without the patience and understanding of my beautiful wife, Emily, and adorable daughter, Maggie. It was the love and support of Emily that allowed me to write and continue to follow a dream. I would like to thank my wife's parents, Bob and Debbie Lamb. Your belief and faith in me over the last several years has provided more motivation than I can ever even begin to tell you. I love you both. I would also like to thank Kenny Roda for the usage of his personal picture collection. Thank you to Jim Friguglietti for his continued guidance and friendship. I would also like to thank Mary Schmitt Boyer for taking the time to read the original manuscript and write a foreword for it, as well as Craig Ehlo, Larry Nance, Austin Carr and Fred McLeod. A big thank-you to Jerry Mires of the *Sports Fix* for his continued support and help over the years. Most importantly, I would like to thank my lord and savior Jesus Christ. It is through your light that all work is done.

Introduction

This story highlights the best moments, players and media members in Cleveland Cavaliers history. It has in-depth, extremely personal interviews with some of the top names in the history of the organization. It is a no-holds-barred account of the most intimate and sometimes controversial details of the most impactful moments in Cavaliers history. This book has input from the players mixed in with the media who covered the Cavs and the fans who watched them. This book will change the way the entire sports nation looks at Cleveland. Finally, the true stories are told!

Chapter 1

The Beginning

In 1970, Cleveland businessman Nick Mileti created the NBA professional expansion team known as the Cleveland Cavaliers. Part of an ownership group, he spent $3.7 million of his own money to bring professional basketball back to Cleveland. Mileti grew up in Cleveland and attended college at Bowling Green State University. He went on to open a profitable law firm, which earned him the funds necessary to purchase the Cleveland Barons hockey team and the building in which they played, the Cleveland Arena.

Mileti knew that the struggling Barons franchise would need a co-tenant and decided to create the Cavaliers. His first act of business was to hire Bill Fitch as the head coach. Fitch had coached in the college ranks, but this would be his first venture into the pro level. He had his work cut out for him with the expansion Cavs.

The team would don sharp-looking wine-and-gold uniforms, although some insist they were maroon and gold. Either way, the jerseys looked nice and had the city buzzing about pro basketball in Cleveland.

The team got off to a slow start by losing its first fifteen games before securing its first win by beating the Portland Trailblazers on November 12, 1970, by a score of 105–103. The Cavs followed the win by losing their next twelve after that and falling to a league-worst 1-27 record. It was all part of a long season that saw them endure several growing pains. They ended the season with a dismal 15-67 record.

However, despite the lousy record, there were several bright spots with which to build for the future. Young and talented players such as Bobby

The Cavaliers entered the NBA in 1970. *Photo by Sam Bourquin.*

Pop star Usher is a partial owner of the team. *Photo by Stephanie Najar.*

Austin Carr has always had a great game face. *Photo by Kenny Roda.*

"Bingo" Smith, who averaged fifteen points a game, would be key building pieces for the future. The bad record also gave the Cavs the first pick in the upcoming draft at the end of the season. All eyes were on the man who eventually became known as Mr. Cavalier.

Austin Carr was a six-foot, four-inch shooting guard out of the University of Notre Dame. He performed incredibly in college, averaging 34.5 points per game, good enough for fifth all-time in college basketball history at the time of his departure. Carr achieved several NCAA tournament records, including most points in one game, most field goals in one game and most field goals attempted in one game. He is widely regarded as one of the top twenty-five college players of all time.

Carr explains the emotions he felt after being drafted by the Cavaliers:

> *It was a joy because I finally realized one of my dreams, which was playing professional basketball. Once I accomplished my degree, pro ball was the next step I wanted to reach. Being drafted number one was an honor, and it was something that I really cherished. It was the second year of the franchise, and my intention was to be on a team that could develop a winning attitude. I wanted to help get things going and keep things going.*

We started that, and then the great teams after us helped keep it going, as far as something being positive basketball wise in Cleveland.

Unfortunately for the Cavs, Carr's first season was hampered by a series of injuries that limited his production. During the 1971 pre-season, he broke his foot and missed the first month of the season. Less than one month after returning to the court, he was sidelined again by another foot injury, causing him to miss another seven weeks. When he returned, he began to display the skills that made him the top selection in the NBA draft and was named to the 1972 All-Rookie Team. The addition of Carr helped the Cavs improve their previous season win total by eight games to finish with a record of 23-59.

The following season saw the Cavaliers continue to improve as their win total grew once again. They used the combination of Carr, Smith and Jim Cleamons to win thirty-two games, which was nearly a double-digit improvement from the previous season. It was a sign that the Cavaliers were headed in the right direction.

The Cavaliers did endure a slight hiccup the following season by winning only twenty-nine games; however, their young talent continued to improve with the addition of rookie Jim Brewer. The Cavs were on the cusp of bigger and better things, including a move into a new venue. The luck of the Cavaliers was about to change, as the team and its fans were about to witness a miracle.

Chapter 2

The Miracle

The Richfield Coliseum was built in the early 1970s and opened to the public in 1974 as the home of the Cleveland Cavaliers. It also played host to the WHA's Cleveland Crusaders, the NHL's Cleveland Barons and, in later years, the AFL's Cleveland Thunderbolts, as well as indoor soccer teams the Cleveland Force and Cleveland Crunch.

The coliseum hosted major sporting events, such as the 1981 NBA All-Star Game. It also showcased several professional wrestling events seen worldwide on pay-per-view. It was the venue for concerts with big names ranging from Frank Sinatra and Stevie Wonder to U2 and Bruce Springsteen. Hall of Fame basketball star Larry Bird even mentioned that it was his favorite place to play on the road. The building, located in the middle of large areas of farmland thirty minutes south of downtown Cleveland, stuck out like a sore thumb. It was a massive structure that held over twenty thousand fans. It was even one of the first arenas to include luxury boxes. Joe Tait, the legendary announcer for the Cavaliers, remembers his first impressions of the Richfield Coliseum:

> *It was a beautiful building in comparison to the old Cleveland Arena; it was like going from the ghetto to the palace. The one question was if people would still show up because of the long distance many had to travel to get there. At the time, that part of Summit County was surrounded by farms. It was in the middle of nowhere, and there was a sheep ranch right next to the building. I thought it was an absolutely beautiful building.*

Jim Chones and Bingo Smith sign autographs. *Photo by Betty Cantley.*

Campy Russell rejoined the team years later as an announcer. *Photo by Sam Bourquin.*

The Cleveland Cavaliers had a new home—now they just needed to start winning. While playing at the Cleveland Arena, the Cavs didn't enjoy much success. Since its opening season of 1970, the team hadn't had a single winning season. Shortly after the move to Richfield in 1974, however, the Cavs' record started to improve. They won forty games that year, falling just short of the playoffs. Joe Tait recalls the 1974–75 season:

> *Things were changing because we were starting to get better ballplayers. We had not yet won a lot of ballgames in the history of the team, so the upgrade in the talent of the roster was crucial. The fact that we came within one game was frustrating but also encouraging because it showed you how close they were to bigger and better things.*

In 1975–76, NBA Coach of the Year Bill Fitch led the Cavaliers to a record of 49-33 and a Central Division title. The team boasted a roster filled with talent such as Austin Carr, Bobby "Bingo" Smith, Jim Chones, Dick Snyder and newly acquired perennial all-star Nate Thurmond. Years had passed since Cleveland had won anything; 1964 was the last time that a Cleveland team won a championship. Thus, the Cavs' success had everyone in northeast Ohio excited about sports again, including announcer Joe Tait:

> *After the horrible start to the season, head coach Bill Fitch made the trade for Nate Thurmond, which was the catalyst that turned that ball club around. Nate was a great player and also a tremendous leader. He came in and really galvanized the team to get them aimed in the right direction and then went on to win the division.*

The first unit of the Cavaliers consisted of Jim Cleamons and Dick Snyder at guard, Jim Chones at center and Jim Brewer and Bobby "Bingo" Smith holding up the frontcourt. Coming off the bench were Austin Carr, Campy Russell, Foots Walker and Nate Thurmond. The bench players were just as good as some of the starting lineups that season. The Cavaliers boasted a solid rotation of players that would to take them well into the post-season.

The enthusiasm of the Cavs' fans helped "lift up" and shape some of the broadcasting by Joe Tait as well. Joe recalls the fan's excitement:

> *Sure, you get swept up in the enthusiasm and excitement of the whole thing. If anything, you have to make sure that you don't overdo it yourself because it is very easy to do so. I know a couple of times listening back to old tapes*

that I probably did go too far. It was hard not to get totally involved in that series because of the extreme nail-biting results of those games. The crowd really did pick up the team, and they picked me up as well. It was a rare experience because it was the first time the team had ever been to the playoffs. They took out Washington, and because most people considered the fact that they were even there a miracle, the name stuck.

The Cavs' first playoff matchup took place against the Washington Bullets, who later became the Washington Wizards. The Bullets were quality opponents who boasted a lineup of all-stars, including Elvin Hayes and Wes Unseld, both of whom went on to become Hall of Famers. (The Bullets' lineup was so formidable that they would go on to win the NBA championship the following season.) The Cavaliers were known for their quick offense and well-rounded attack on both sides of the ball. They would need all of that to take down the Bullets. With Joe Tait on the microphone, calling the action to hungry sports fans everywhere, the series was ready to kick off with a bang.

Game One ended in heartbreak for the Cavaliers as they lost in front of the hometown crowd, 100–95. They bounced back in Game Two, played in Washington, by defeating the Bullets by a score of 80–79 on a twenty-five-foot jump shot by Bobby "Bingo" Smith in the final seconds of the game. The one-point win in thrilling fashion was a sign of things to come later in the series. The boys in wine and gold kept the momentum going in Game Three with a hard-fought win in Richfield, outscoring the Bullets 88–76. Desperate for a win back home in Game Four, the Bullets would find one with a 109–98 victory. The Cavaliers won Game Five at home, 92–91, when Jimmy Cleamons was able to rebound a Smith shot and put it back in to beat the buzzer. The series grew more exciting and intense by the day. Game Six went to overtime, but the Bullets managed to bounce back again by winning 102–98.

There are few moments in sports that can match the buildup and thrill of a Game Seven. The feeling of "do or die" is one of pure anxiety that can be cured only with a win. The ground of the Richfield Coliseum was shaking up to an hour before the game as the fans yelled in excitement. During warm-ups, the crowd of twenty-thousand-plus chanted, "Let's go Cavs!" If the fans had anything to do with it, the Cavaliers would not be having a first-round exit. Joe Tait had a special viewpoint of the fans' reaction from the broadcast table on the court:

Austin Carr went from the court to the broadcast booth. *Photo by Sam Bourquin.*

Sportswriter Vince McKee with the Miracle of Richfield team. *Courtesy of www.vpeterpress.com.*

It was a "natural" crowd reaction, and that is what made it so special. Nate Thurmond had his brother, George, come to one of the games and place a tape recorder on his lap so he could record the amazing sound of the crowd at the packed Coliseum. There had never been anything like what we were all experiencing. That entire season, the crowd response was just unbelievable. Those things don't happen anymore because of the artificial commercial atmosphere produced at arenas now.

As fate would have it, Game Seven would be an even more intense game than the previous six thrillers that the fans had witnessed. Just like in previous games, it once again came down to the final moments, as Dick Snyder was called on to take the final shot with just under five seconds remaining. As his running five-foot bank shot hit off the glass and went in, the Richfield crowd came unglued. The city had just witnessed the completion of a miracle.

Although the Cavs would fall short in the next round of the playoffs, losing to the highly touted Boston Celtics in six games, no one could take away the pure joy Cleveland fans felt during Game Seven of the Bullets series. Many believe that if starting center Jim Chones hadn't been hurt in a practice between the two series, the Cavaliers might have even upset the Celtics. Chones had broken his foot during a practice and was forced to sit out, taking the steam out of the red-hot locomotive engine that had become Cavaliers basketball. The Cavs did manage to win two games in the series with outstanding play at home in front of the rabid fans. Backup center Nate Thurmond did his best to fill in for Chones; however, John Havlicek was too much for him. Joe Tait relates his firsthand view of what happened during the games against Boston:

Nobody expected the Cavaliers to beat Boston at that particular time, and the fact that they came back in that series got people pumped up to an even higher level. People began to think that even without Chones, this team could still be a team of destiny. It was in the fans' minds that they could pull off one of the all-time great upsets. It was easy for the fans to get swept away in it. The problem was that Thurmond had to pick up extra minutes for the hurt Chones, and it was simply too much to ask. Despite their best efforts, we fell short in six games.

Austin Carr reflects back on that magical time in Cavaliers history:

That was the best basketball team I have ever played on. Not just talent-wise but also personality-wise, as I'm still close friends with them today.

Sportswriter Vince McKee with Campy Russell. *Courtesy of www.vpeterpress.com.*

When I first got to the Cavs, we had to weed out all the guys with personal goals, and once we got them out of the way, we were able to focus as a team on winning as a team. That is how we came together, and the city embraced us for it. We were very close the year before as we only missed the playoffs by one game. We played hard and as a team every night—our losses weren't for a lack of effort. The city embraced us because of the hard work ethic that we showed on a nightly basis. We started off that season at 6-11, and then we got Nate Thurmond and took off winning games. I really believe that if Jim Chones never got injured, we would have won the championship. We worked hard, and everyone in the league knew it, too. Everything happens for a reason, and we just couldn't get over the hump. We were a well-oiled machine, as everyone knew their role and played it well. Once you took a guy out of the rotation, it kind of messed up how we functioned. We were ten men deep, and our locker room was loaded with great human beings. If someone said something to you as a teammate in the locker room, you didn't take it personal; you just tried to do it better the next time. That is a winning formula—to have guys who can correct themselves. We knew that if we ever lost two games in a row, we didn't even need to say anything. The third game we would be bringing it, and bringing it strong.

The truth was that Cleveland sports teams were in the midst of a miserable run. The Browns hadn't been good in years. The Indians never made it back to the playoffs after getting swept in the World Series in 1954 against the San Francisco Giants. The Cavaliers had struggled until this magical run. It gave the city some hope it desperately needed. It didn't matter if it was the clever nicknames or the colorful uniforms, Cleveland fans were just happy to have a winner.

Chapter 3
The Lost Years

With basketball fever reaching an all-time high following the Miracle of Richfield team, the city of Cleveland was abuzz heading into the 1976–77 season. The Cavs had an exciting and young team set to return to the court. They were led by Austin Carr, Campy Russell and Bingo Smith, all averaging over fifteen points a game. With a 44-39 record, Bill Fitch was able to lead them back to the playoffs, where they faced their rival from the previous season, the Washington Bullets.

This year was unlike the Miracle year, as this time Washington was loaded with talent and would not be denied. The Cavs fought hard but surrendered the series to the Bullets in three close games. The Bullets won Game One by a score of 109–100. The Cavs battled back to win Game Two, outscoring the high-powered Bullets 91–83. The series was knotted up at a game apiece when they reached the decisive Game Three. (The NBA had added extra teams to the playoffs that season, which caused the first round to be shortened to only three games.) The Bullets closed out the series with a 104–98 win.

The Cavaliers kept their momentum rolling as they entered the 1977–78 season. They did it with the help of players such as Campy Russell, who led the team with nineteen points a game. They also had the assistance of key free-agent pickup Walt Frazier, who proved he still had plenty of gas left in the tank by averaging sixteen points a game. Jim Chones continued to control the paint by pulling down more than ten rebounds a game. Foots Walker led the team in assists with over 450 for the season. The Bill Fitch–led squad returned to the playoffs for the third straight season, finishing with a

Sportswriter Vince McKee with radio play-by-play man Mike Snyder. *Courtesy of www. vpeterpress.com.*

43-39 record. They managed to avoid facing Washington for a third straight season; however, they ran into the equally hot New York Knicks. The Knicks were a strong opponent and led by such all-stars as Bob McAdoo and Earl Monroe. The Cavaliers were swept out of the playoffs in two straight games after losses of 132–114 and 109–107.

Despite the back-to-back first-round playoff exits, the Cavaliers had been showing promise, and the young nucleus needed to contend for several years ahead. That is why fans were so shocked when the Cavs digressed so poorly in the 1978–79 season, finishing with a 30-52 record. It was the first time in years that they had finished below .500 and missed the playoffs.

Stan Albeck took over for Bill Fitch as coach to start the 1979–80 season. The coaching switch didn't help matters, however, as the Cavs finished under .500 again with a 37-45 record. It was the second straight season the Cavaliers had missed the playoffs after three straight years of appearing in them. Sadly for Cavaliers fans, things were about to get worse.

In 1980, a dark spell was cast over Cleveland basketball when Ted Stepien purchased the Cavaliers. He was the founder of Nationwide Advertising Services and thought his knowledge of advertising could transfer over to being a successful basketball franchise owner. While some may have applauded him for his ambition, many more despised him for almost ruining basketball in Cleveland.

It wasn't long into his ownership that many around the NBA were saying that his franchise was one of the most poorly run in all of sports. If he had any fans after inventing a dance team called the Teddy Bears, he promptly lost them when he fired popular announcer Joe Tait. When he wasn't concerning himself with dancers and announcers, Stepien was going through a carousel of head coaches. He initially hired Bill Mussleman from the University of Minnesota in the hope that he could turn the team around. His faith in Mussleman proved to be fruitless, however, and he fired him a short time later. After this failed experiment, he went on to hire and fire Don Delaney, Bob Kloppenburg and Chuck Daly before once again giving the head coaching job to Mussleman. In only a few seasons, he had turned the franchise into one of the biggest jokes in sports. Not long after that, fans started calling the team the "Cleveland Cadavers."

If Stepien's handling of head coaches wasn't bad enough, things with the team grew worse when he proceeded to trade away high draft picks for mediocre players. The most notable mistake is when he traded the team's top draft pick to the Los Angeles Lakers, who went on to pick future Hall of Famer James Worthy. Stepien's outlandish behavior prompted the NBA to create a rule, called "Stepien's Rule," stating that a team couldn't trade away its top draft pick two years in a row. Attendance at Cavaliers games dropped drastically under his ownership, prompting him to start looking for answers. One of these was switching the name to the Ohio Cavaliers and having them play their home games in multiple arenas, some not even located in Ohio. In just three seasons as owner, Stepien managed to compile a record of 66-180. He was set to move the team to Toronto when the Gund brothers stepped in and bought the team.

Gordon Gund and his brother, George, were born into success because their dad, Gordon II, was the president of Cleveland Trust Bank, one of the biggest banks in Ohio at the time. They grew up with a sense of passion and urgency when it came to succeeding at any level. Gordon was born on October 15, 1939, and grew up learning from his father what it took to be successful not only in business but also in life. Gordon Gund had done plenty to help local charities. At the time of the Cavs sale, Mr. Gund's philanthropic deeds were not in the media spotlight. He preferred his charity work to go unnoticed by the media and public.

Gordon was also no stranger to high academic standards and discipline, as he had attended Groton School, a five-year private Episcopalian college prep school in Massachusetts. The school is famous as one of the top boarding schools in New England and doesn't admit many students. On average, it hosts only 350 to 400 students for all five grades offered. It is considered by many to be one of the nation's top twenty-five college prep schools. It was no surprise when Gordon graduated and attended Harvard University, where he majored in physical sciences. Splitting his time between the classroom and the hockey rink, young Gordon breezed through college. After graduation, he joined the U.S. Navy. It became crystal clear that he was a born leader when he ascended to command two separate destroyers. He continued to show his leadership ability after leaving the navy by following in his father's footsteps and working in the banking industry in corporate finance. He would continue to excel despite suffering from retinitis pigmentosa, a degenerative eye disease that causes severe blindness. He would later create the Retinitis Pigmentosa Foundation to help raise money and fight the horrible disease.

The Gund brothers had already owned the Richfield Coliseum, and it seemed like a natural move for them to purchase the venue's main revenue producer, the Cleveland Cavaliers. It didn't take them long to shake things up by changing the team's colors from wine and gold to orange and blue. They also replaced the swordsman mascot with the word "Cavs," with the "v" stylized as a net. The changes were small but made a huge impact on the direction of the franchise for years to come. It was a new era in Cleveland basketball, one that would give everybody hope.

Gund brought in George Karl to be the head coach starting in the 1984–85 season. Karl inherited a group of aging veterans and unproven youngsters. He knew he would have a tall task on his hands, and that became clear as the Cavs lost nineteen of their first twenty-one games. Starting the season with such a horrible record would have been a death sentence for most teams; however, this team had heart and was led by a colorful character named Lloyd B. Free, or, as fans would come to know him, World B. Free. He would go on to become one of the most colorful and well-remembered players in Cleveland Cavaliers history.

Free had received his nickname years earlier while playing in Brooklyn because of his forty-four-inch vertical leap and 360-degree dunks. He was known for taking high-profile shots and playing flamboyantly. He was a proven scorer and had already surpassed fifteen thousand career points by the time he arrived in Cleveland for his ninth NBA season. Free was loved by his teammates and fans alike, and between his energy and the steady leadership of George Karl, the Cavaliers managed to right the ship and win thirty-six games before season's end. It was a down year for the Eastern

Conference, and the low win total was actually just enough to squeeze the Cavs back into the playoffs. They would eventually lose to the dominant Boston Celtics; however, just the fact that they had made it to the playoffs after such a horrible start was a major accomplishment. It was a perfect example of a team overcoming horrible odds, never giving up and pushing through tough times to achieve remarkable things.

Despite the return to the playoffs, George Karl and the Cavaliers could not return to their winning ways in the 1985–86 season. Karl did his best but was fired before season's end. Gene Littles finished the season. The Cavaliers finished with a record of 29-53. The Gunds knew it was time to make a change.

The Gunds were new to the world of professional basketball, so it didn't take them long to get an NBA veteran in their front office to build the team. Wayne Embry was chosen by the Gund brothers to assemble a team that could make a quick turnaround and once again be a playoff contender. Wayne Embry was born in Springfield, Ohio, in 1937. He attended and played basketball for Tecumseh High School and from there went on to play basketball at Miami University (Ohio). He was drafted by the St. Louis Hawks in 1958 before being traded to the Cincinnati Royals. His pro career covered eleven years playing for the Boston Celtics and Milwaukee Bucks. After doing a lot of behind-the-scenes front office work while playing in Milwaukee, he eventually became the NBA's first African American general manager after he retired from being a player. The Milwaukee Bucks made history by having Embry as their GM for seven seasons. After the seven-year run in Milwaukee, Wayne decided that it was a time to take a break and stepped away from the game for a few years. In 1986, the Gund brothers brought him to Cleveland to begin building a dynasty. This move spoke volumes for the Gunds' convincing strengths and would be a key part in the rebuilding process. Every large ship needs a captain to steer it, and the Gunds found their captain in Embry.

Chapter 4

The Lenny Wilkens Era

Wayne Embry's first move was to bring in a coach to help guide the team. His choice was Lenny Wilkens, a man who would eventually go down as one of the greatest basketball coaches of all time. Wilkens was born on October 28, 1937, in Brooklyn, New York. He graduated from Providence College, where he was a two-time all-American, even leading his team to its first appearance in the NIT tournament. His collegiate career was so impressive that years later, in 1996, the school decided to retire his number fourteen jersey. At the time of his graduation, Wilkens was the second all-time leading scorer in school history. His college career was a sign of things to come, both on the court and on the sidelines.

Lenny followed up an impressive college career with an even better professional stint in the NBA. He was drafted by the St. Louis Hawks in 1960 and went on to play eight seasons for them. In his rookie year with the Hawks, they made the championship round, losing to the Boston Celtics. Perhaps his most impressive season was in 1967–68, when he finished second to the great Wilt Chamberlain in MVP voting. Many people feel that Wilkens's season was actually better than Chamberlain's, but voters valued scoring more than they did team play. Wilkens was the all-around best player in the league.

In a surprising move, the Hawks dealt Wilkens to the Seattle Supersonics in 1968 for Walt Hazzard. Wilkens was named head coach while still playing for the Seattle Supersonics prior to the 1969–70 season. He was able to perform well even with the added pressure of coaching as he made the All-

Sportswriter Vince McKee with Larry Nance. *Courtesy of www.vpeterpress.com.*

Star team three more times during his days with Seattle. Not only did the team's record improve under the direction of Wilkens, but he also managed to average twenty-plus points, six-plus rebounds and eight assists during his playing days there. Those statistics would be great for any player, let alone one who was also focusing his time on coaching.

Wilkens was traded from Seattle to Cleveland in 1972. He spent two seasons with the Cavaliers before finishing his career with the Portland Trailblazers. He retired as a Trailblazer after the 1974–75 season and then went on to coach with them for the 1976 season. His stints in Seattle and Cleveland were short, but both cities instantly grew to love Wilkens because of his work ethic and superior knowledge of the game.

When his playing career was finished, Wilkens would be considered one of the best of all time. A nine-time all-star and the MVP of the 1971 All-Star Game, he was voted into the Naismith Memorial Basketball Hall of Fame in 1989. He was masterful at both scoring and assists. He showed how he was an unselfish teammate by leading the league in assists for the 1969–70 season. His number nineteen was retired by the Seattle Supersonics, and he

Beloved point guard Mark Price. *Photo by Sheryl Scanlon.*

was also voted to the NBA's 50th Anniversary Team. Few could compare to the greatness of Wilkens, and he would become one of the most sought-after coaches upon his retirement from being a full-time player.

Mark Price hits another jumper from the top of the key. *Photo by Sheryl Scanlon*.

Mark Price connects for two more against the Hawks. *Photo by Sheryl Scanlon*.

Wilkens enjoyed his time as a player/coach in both Seattle and Portland. It was only a matter of time after he retired from playing before he would once again roam the sidelines as a coach. He returned to Seattle, replacing Bob Hopkins, a quarter of the way through the 1977–78 season. The team had only five victories at that point in the season, and pressure was placed on Wilkens to turn things around. It didn't take long for him to do so, as the Supersonics began to dramatically improve. They won eleven of their first twelve games under his direction and never looked back. They used the momentum of the winning streak, along with the masterful coaching skills of Wilkens, all the way to the NBA championship series. The Supersonics eventually lost to the talented Washington Bullets in the finals. Despite the loss in the championship, it was a sign that Wilkens would have a long, successful career as a coach. A turnaround of this proportion was almost unheard of; if Wilkens could turn the team around that drastically, that quickly, one could only imagine how well he could do with a full season.

The Supersonics returned to the championship series the very next season. They faced the Washington Bullets again, this time winning the series in a mere five games. The championship was the first and only in Seattle NBA history. Wilkens showed that he could manage a team of all-stars that included Gus Williams, Jack Sikma and finals MVP Dennis Johnson. He also proved he could handle a bench with his use of talented reserves Paul Silas and Fred Brown. Wilkens excelled at playing team ball in his career, and now his main focus on the sideline was to coach and win with the same philosophy. It was an attitude he would eventually bring with him to Cleveland, and it would change the culture of Cavs basketball for many years to come.

When Wilkens left the coaching position in Seattle, it didn't take long for Wayne Embry to offer him a contract coaching the Cavaliers for the 1986–87 season. This move proved the team was headed in the right direction. It also shocked people because Seattle was a winning franchise at the time, and Cleveland was known for losing. The move proved that Wilkens had faith in Embry's ability to bring in talent. With the ownership, general manager and head coach all in place, it would be only a matter of time before winning ways would return to Cleveland. It is vital for a coach to have a say in the players he is given, as well as for the general manager to have a solid understanding of what players will best fit the system laid out by the coach. The fact that Embry and Wilkens were both former players who had excelled in the league only helped matters when it came to finding that mutual understanding of what it took to win on a consistent basis.

Mark Price was unstoppable on many nights. *Photo by Sheryl Scanlon.*

Duke alum Danny Ferry came to the Cavs with high expectations. *Photo by Sheryl Scanlon.*

Craig Ehlo was beloved by many. *Photo by Sheryl Scanlon.*

Cavs players who played under Wilkens described him as one of the smartest and best coaches they ever played for. They respected him because he played the game of basketball and had a true understanding of what it took to win. Wilkens might have been soft-spoken at times, but his words carried great weight. Excellent words of wisdom are the same, no matter whether you are screaming them or whispering them softly. As Larry Nance said:

> *Coach Wilkens understood how to communicate with his players without yelling at them, and that is why he was so successful. We were a great group, and it was because we had the best coach ever. As a person, he was even better because he cared about you and never yelled at you. He was stern and would let you know what you were doing wrong, but then after practice, he would sit down with you and talk about family. He was that kind of coach, and it made it feel like we were part of a family. If I ever coach, or if my children decide to coach, I want them to be identical to that man because he was awesome.*

The Cavalier roster was decent, but it was also in need of improvements in certain areas. The pressure was on Embry to make the proper selections in the upcoming draft. It would also be crucial for him to lure free agents to play in Cleveland. He had the proper coach in place, now he just needed the right mix of players for him to guide. It was crucial that Embry put together the right mix of talent to learn from Lenny Wilkens.

June 17, 1986, is a day that changed the course of history of Cleveland basketball for many years to come. It was on that day that the Cavs drafted Brad Daugherty, a center out of the University of North Carolina, as the first overall pick in the draft. The team had acquired the first pick in a trade the day before that sent Roy Hinson to the Philadelphia 76ers. It was one of the smartest moves in Embry's career as general manager. Seven draft picks later, the Cavaliers selected Ron Harper out of Miami University (Ohio). Both players were highly touted college players. They went on to select Johnny Newman, Kevin Henderson, Warren Martin, Ben Davis, Gilbert Wilburn and Ralph Daulton in the draft as well. Wayne Embry was not done dealing yet on that faithful day, as he would also send a future 1989 second-round draft pick to the Dallas Mavericks in exchange for the draft rights of Mark Price, who was also a first-round pick coming out of the Georgia Institute of Technology. With the acquisition of Price, the Cavaliers now had three first-round talents on the roster. It was a trade that the 76ers would regret for many years to come. The three first-rounders all went on to have stellar

careers, and Roy Hinson never truly achieved what the Philadelphia brass expected from him.

Brad Daugherty, who was born in 1965 in Black Mountain, North Carolina, grew into a seven-foot frame that was destined for the hardwood. Daugherty excelled at basketball while playing at Charles D. Owen High School. With his leadership on the court, his team reached the 1982 state finals before losing in the championship game. His play in high school caught the attention of one of the best college coaches of all time.

Above: Mark Price was widely considered the most popular Cavalier of all time. *Photo by Sheryl Scanlon*.

Top: Mark Price and "Hot Rod" Williams. *Photo by Sheryl Scanlon*.

Brad was a top recruit later that year for Dean Smith and the North Carolina Tar Heels. He would be remembered as one of the few players to play for a Hall of Fame coach in both college and the NBA. Many considered him one of the best centers to ever play for UNC. He was a two-time All-ACC first-team selection and a first-team All-American in his senior season, during which he averaged more than twenty points a game. Based on his impressive college basketball career, Daugherty was inducted into the North Carolina Sports Hall of Fame.

Joining Daugherty on the Cavaliers that year was fellow first-round draft pick Ron Harper, from Miami University (Ohio). Harper had been a collegiate all-star, drawing many comparisons to Dr. J, Julius Erving, for his high-flying style. Harper was a two-time MAC Player of the Year and made the NCAA All-American second team in his senior season. He immediately showed that Embry's faith in him was warranted when he had a great rookie season, averaging over twenty-two points a game. He finished second in the Rookie of the Year voting to Indiana Pacer Chuck Person. The soft-spoken Harper was a favorite among both fans and his teammates. His trade years later would be one of the most shocking and most regretted in Cavs history.

Mark Price was the player in charge of keeping everything running smoothly. A fellow first-round pick of the Dallas Mavericks, he was the perfect man to lead the charge. Price had grown up in Bartlesville, Oklahoma, where he attended Enid High School. After graduating, he went on to play college basketball at Georgia Tech University. With hard work and court savvy, he managed to establish himself as the leader of the team. He was a two-time All-American along with receiving All-ACC honors in all four years of his college career. In the 1984–85 ACC championship game, he led his team to a win over the University of North Carolina and his future teammate Brad Daugherty. He was also named ACC Player of the Year. Price's jersey number at Georgia Tech was retired in acknowledgement of his great college career. So beloved in Cleveland was Price, that in the 2014 off-season, he became one of the leading candidates to replace Mike Brown as head coach.

Joining forces with the top three draft picks was the Cavs' 1985 draft pick, John "Hot Rod" Williams. Legal problems forced Williams to sit out his rookie season after being selected by Cleveland in the draft. He had had a solid career at Tulane University, and Embry and the Cavs were willing to look past his somewhat checkered past and put him fully into the fold. Williams had an impressive build and great ability to find rebounds and block shots. Embry knew that if he could put his troubled past behind him, he could be a force on the court and a key part of what Wilkens was trying to do with the new ball club. Larry Nance discloses how it was to play with "Hot Rod" Williams:

He was very underrated as one of the best low-post defensive players that have ever been around. He was a great defensive guy and also a great friend. Once you're his friend, he will do anything in the world for you. We became great friends, and we still talk today.

Midway through the 1986–87 season, Embry decided to sign free agent guard Craig Ehlo. Ehlo reflects on growing up learning the game:

There was only one game a week on television when I was growing up, so I didn't really have any one athlete I molded myself after. The most influential person in my life who helped me with basketball was my high school coach, Joe Mahaga, at Monterrey. He was influential in teaching me the fundamentals of the game. He taught us a continuity-type offense, where we would pass the ball about six times before we got anything to look at shot-wise. I was blessed in that area because he was determined to teach us the strict fundamentals and the teamwork part of the game, which helped me develop as a player. At six feet, four inches tall, I wasn't a very big kid in high school, so I had to find ways to perform well with using my size against larger opponents. My junior college coach, Ron Mayberry, was also very influential in helping me develop every aspect of my game. I was built to be a swing-type player because I could handle the ball and shoot the ball well at my size."

Ehlo went to college at Odessa Junior College and then transferred to Washington State. He reflects on that time in his life and his basketball career:

My high school team made it to the regional championships in Texas, and I was lucky enough to lead my team in scoring. However, I think my size may have deterred any school from recruiting me. I didn't have a lot of offers out of high school even though my team was successful. I did have a few accolades such as being All-State and things like that. I just chose junior college because it was a better avenue for me and close to my home in Lubbock, Texas. I went down there for two years, and that was a big part of my life because I was able to put on some more weight. It allowed me to play more and get better as I played 36 games my freshman year and 31 my sophomore year. I was able to average about 24 points a game my sophomore year, with 6 rebounds a game and 7 assists. I think that is what caught the attention of several schools. I received letters from the University of Texas, University of Houston, Oklahoma, Iowa, and some other smaller schools such as Baylor and SMU. It was Washington State that caught my attention the most because at the time, the PAC 10 was a dominant conference. I felt that it was a chance to play in one of the nation's premiere conferences. I had a great coach in George Raveling. He taught me a tremendous amount of respect for the game. He taught me how to use my skills, and we were able to finish my senior season in second place in the PAC 10. We only lost by one game to UCLA and were ranked fourth in the country at that time. We made it to the NCAA tournament and beat Weber State in the first round before losing to the University of Virginia in the second round.

In 1983, Ehlo was drafted by the Houston Rockets, where he played for three years in a limited role. Ehlo explains that the draft back then was much different than the draft today:

The draft was not celebrated and exposed as it is today with ESPN covering the whole thing. I was at Washington State working at our summer camps when the draft was happening. I was on an outdoor court helping out with some young children, chasing them around, when the camp director came and told me I was drafted by Houston in the third round. I didn't do much celebrating; instead I just went back to work at the camp. That was when they had rookie camps in the middle of the summer, and then we would get invited to the veterans' camp after that. I made that team for the first three years under one-year contracts each time. It was like $40,000 coming out of a college, and I thought I was a very rich man.

After his third season, Ehlo was able to move into free agency, allowing Embry to sign him. The Rockets reached the NBA Finals in 1986 before losing to the perennial powerhouse Boston Celtics. Ehlo's playoff experience made him even more inviting to the Cleveland Cavs' organization. Ehlo shares how it felt to play for the Rockets and in that championship series against the Celtics:

In the next year's draft, we selected Hakeem Olajuwon, and he completed the twin towers that the team had, so I didn't play a lot. I only got into a handful of games, but I can say I was part of the 12-man roster that beat the Lakers in five games in the conference finals before losing to Larry Bird, Kevin McHale and those guys in the finals. That was the Celtics' year, as they went 40-1 at home and just couldn't be beat; we hung in there but lost in six games. The last game was a blowout, and I got to play the last few minutes and be out there to score the last basket before the fans rushed the court. That was my one brief moment in the NBA Finals.

Ehlo explains his decision to sign with Cleveland midway through the 1986–87 season:

My coach in Houston was Bill Fitch, who was one of the first Cleveland coaches. Cleveland did not have a good team at that point, so coach Fitch would always tease us and say, "I'm going to send you to Cleveland" when we weren't playing well. I was in the Western Conference and only had to go to Cleveland once, and that was when the Coliseum was out there, so I wasn't familiar with Cleveland at all. I grew up a Dallas Cowboys fan, so I was somewhat familiar with the Browns. I knew that Cleveland fans were a very sports-minded group of people. I got signed to a ten-day contract with the Cavs when Mark Price came down with tendonitis. Coach Wilkens was familiar with me from coaching in Seattle when I was at Washington State. I had talked with him several times when I was doing the rookie camps. When Bagley went down with a sprained ankle, it left me with a few others to play as the guards. It was a baptism by fire. We played 5 games in the 10 days I was there, which gave me a chance to perform for them. I was able to sign with them for the rest of the year after that stint. It was a weird way of getting to Cleveland, but I'm very glad that I did get there. I was brought up to be loyal and to keep your word, and when Houston had called me asking me to come, I knew that even though it would have been easy to go back to Houston, I had given my word to Cleveland and owed it to them to stay there and start fresh.

The 1986–87 season was a learning and growing experience for the Cavs, which upper management had expected. The team finished with only thirty-one wins but showed growth in many ways. John Williams, Brad Daugherty and Ron Harper all made the NBA All-Rookie team. Despite the sixth-place finish, the rookies' playing skills gave Cleveland fans hope.

The 1987–88 season brought low expectations from many outside of the Cavs organization. The team had gotten off to a mediocre start before Embry pulled the trigger on a blockbuster deal that brought seasoned veteran Larry Nance to town. On February 25, 1988, the Cavs traded away Tyrone Korbin, Kevin Johnson, Mark West and two future draft picks to the Phoenix Suns. In exchange, Phoenix sent Larry Nance, Mike Sanders and a future first-round pick to Cleveland.

Nance's acquisition was seen by many in the media as placing the final piece in the Cavs' rebuilding puzzle. Larry Nance grew up in Anderson, South Carolina, the youngest in a large family of great athletes. He learned the game of basketball from his brothers, cousins and uncles. At first, his older relatives would not allow him to play with them because he was too small, but then, as he grew older—and taller—he became very talented, and the family allowed him to play all the time. He spent most of his childhood on the court with his family learning to play and perfecting his skills.

Nance grew up idolizing the great Julius Erving. He was glued to his television every time he had the chance to watch him play. He spent every Sunday afternoon in his own backyard, which he named "The Spectrum," pretending to be Dr. J. Nance would later say that Dr. J was his favorite player until he reached the NBA and played against his idol.

Nance went to a trade school in McDuffie, South Carolina, following in the footsteps of his father, who was a truck driver. While studying basic academics at the school, he also played basketball. Anderson Junior College recruited him to play for a year, but then Nance was recruited by Clemson. Clemson head coach Bill Foster had already seen Nance play and offered Larry the last "available" scholarship. His faith in Nance was strong, and he knew that he would be more than worth taking the chance on. It was a loss for Anderson Junior College, as it lost a top recruit, but choosing Clemson over Anderson was a no-brainer for Nance. It is not often that a major ACC college would happen to have an extra scholarship. Call it fate or whatever, but for Nance and Clemson, it was the start of a beautiful partnership. Following a good career at Clemson, Nance was picked by the Phoenix Suns in the first round of the 1981 NBA draft. He reflects on the excitement and emotion of being drafted by Phoenix:

> *To come from a small town like Anderson, it felt really good because making the pros was never a realistic expectation growing up. I just loved to play basketball, and I loved playing hard. And because of playing hard, things worked out. When I realized I was going to get the opportunity to go to Phoenix and play, it was just awesome. Upon arriving in the pros, I continued to play the only way that I know how to play, and that's just*

work hard and try to develop to make myself better. That approach turned out a successful basketball career.

It didn't take Nance long to blossom into a superstar, as he participated and won the 1984 Slam Dunk Championship contest, following in the high-flying footsteps of his hero, Dr. J, Julius Erving. The trade that eventually brought Nance to Cleveland would go down as one of the signature moves of the Wayne Embry era. However, it was a rough trade at first for Nance. As he explains:

> *At the time, it was the worst thing that could happen to me because I loved playing in Phoenix, plus I loved racecars and was able to get to the track several times a week. I was under the impression that if you played hard and kept your nose clean, you would always be with the same team. The night I got traded, I was upset because it was cold in Cleveland. There were two places I never wanted to play, and they were Cleveland and New York. It was the worst time in my life—I was filled with pressure because I was supposed to bring the change. Then I met my new teammates, and things began to change. I started to be around them and play with them, and I realized what great people they were. And with the great coaches that we had, things started changing, we started winning. All of a sudden, this trade turned out to be the best thing in my life. I became best friends with "Hot Rod." We became a very successful team with a great point guard. Things just began to work out better, and I became very happy to be here.*

The Cavs played well for the final twenty-seven games of the season because of Nance's addition. They ended the season with a modest 42-40 record, finishing fifth in the Eastern Conference Central Division. They made the playoffs for the first time in several years, where they lost to Chicago in the first round, taking the Bulls to the limit by forcing a deciding Game Five in the best-of-five series. It was the first trip to the playoffs for this young group and also their first showdown with a player who would become a familiar enemy, Michael Jordan.

The Cavs didn't care about who the leading scorer was each night. Their philosophy was to feed the hot hand on any given night. They were unselfish, which was a key component to their winning. There weren't any egos on the team, a true sign of teamwork and great coaching. Longtime radio play-by-play man Joe Tait shares the following about the Cavs' team dynamics:

That was a ballclub from top to bottom. It was a more talented team than the Miracle team, but on the same token, the league was much better as well. Michael Jordan was playing in a league of his own. You had Isaiah Thomas with the Pistons, Malone and Stockton with the Jazz and the best pound-for-pound player, Magic Johnson, who could play all five positions. It was the same in the standpoint that the fans really got pumped. But on the same token, the league was loaded with talented teams at that particular time.

It was common for the Cavs to have a two-hour practice, followed by a one-hour meeting in the locker room. They loved to talk and spend time with one another so much that after most practices, they would all go over to a teammate's house to bond some more. Larry Nance shares his view of this magical time:

I think it is because we loved each other and it didn't matter night to night who was the leading scorer. We didn't care who was going to be the leading scorer; we just wanted to win. Our goal was to find the guys with the hot hands and keep feeding them the ball. There were no egos ever, anywhere or anytime! We never got into an argument about someone taking too many shots—it just never happened. We truly loved being around each other, and so did our wives and families. I was never part of a group that was like that before or after. That kind of teamwork and chemistry is what made us successful. I don't see that type of thing anymore with today's athletes and teams. That's why when I go places, so many people say they loved our group. They enjoyed watching unselfish team basketball.

This team bond was very rare in professional sports. Craig Ehlo tries to explain the chemistry of the team during this time:

The main thing was team chemistry and that we made ourselves available for fans by living in the local area. Our chemistry was built with several factors in place, one of which was the fact that Larry Nance had a pond behind his house that we would go fishing in before practice. We played together, and it didn't matter that we had all-stars because we still played together. I think people really enjoyed our team because of the team ball method of playing. It didn't matter who led the team in scoring as long as we won. I think it was a fun time for people to come out and watch a team play together like that. Then in the off-season, we all stayed in town and none of us moved out of state. I lived in Fairlawn, Mark and Brad lived in Hudson, Larry lived in Bath and "Hot Rod" lived in Akron, so we were visible. We would go to Summit Mall and constantly interact with fans. I think because we were visible and stayed in the community throughout the year it helped the fans' relationship with us. I think it helped having Joe Tait around because if he was doing something with his horses at the racetracks or events with women's groups, it was amazing. I never thought I would spend my summers in Cleveland, but then I found that there was lots to do by sticking around. There were plenty of golf courses and many other things to do. I think our visibility in the community is what won over the hearts of the fans.

Ehlo goes on to explain how everyone on the team got along so well together:

Our wives would get mad at us after the games because we would sit in the shower for over an hour after the game like a bunch of old women just talking. We would walk out in that cold garage in the Richfield Coliseum, and our wives would be like, "What is taking you so long?" It was just an amazing time listening to "Hot Rod" talking about Louisiana or Larry talking about cars, or even listening to Tree Rollins talk about how many kids he had. Garry Briggs, our trainer, was the glue that held us together.

The fans flocked to the Coliseum to see this unique and unselfish team-orientated basketball. The Coliseum was rocking nightly as the fans gravitated to the players on the court because of their workman-like approach. The total season attendance in 1987–88 was 730,925, a number good enough to finish fifth out of twenty-five teams in the league. It proved once again that when Cleveland produces a winner, the fans show up to the games.

The 1988–89 season was the first full season with the core team in place, and it quickly showed as the Cavs continued to improve. They managed to win a club-record fifty-seven games, good enough to finish second in the Eastern Conference Central Division. The key factor to the improvement was how well the team bonded. They were friends on and off the court and truly cared for one another. This was a factor in building their chemistry and made them dangerous to any opponent.

The first-round playoff matchup that season was against the Chicago Bulls, a team the Cavs had beaten all six times they faced them in the regular season. With home court advantage and the dominant regular-season record in place, it seemed that the Cavs would easily get revenge for the previous season's playoff outcome. Sadly, with expectations high, they promptly lost Game One of the series at home, 88–95. However, they bounced back with a 96–88 Game Two victory and traveled to Chicago with the series tied. The Bulls wasted no time in reclaiming the lead in the series with a 101–94 Game Three win. A thrilling Game Four overtime win for the Cavs sent the series back home to Cleveland for the fifth and decisive game.

In Game Five, Craig Ehlo played the game of his life, scoring twenty-four points (including four three-pointers) and four assists off the bench, and gave the Chicago defenders fits all afternoon. His go-ahead layup in the last few seconds of the game gave the Cavs a 100–99 lead. Then, Chicago called its last timeout to set up a final play. Seconds later, Michael Jordan hit "the shot," and Cleveland was knocked out of the playoffs for the second straight year by the greatest basketball player of all time. Jordan finished with a game-high forty-four points, and his game-winning shot would go down as one of the most famous of all time. Larry Nance relates why, after such a great season, things went wrong in the playoffs:

> *Not to make excuses, because the team from Chicago was very good, but injuries hurt us late in the season. I know I had some ankle problems that may have held me out of the next round. I truly feel that when our team was healthy, we could beat any team in the league, including Chicago. I'm not making excuses; I'm just saying we weren't healthy, and they went on to win. It's just part of life in basketball.*

Craig Ehlo shares what he thinks happened during that playoff run:

> *We just owned the Bulls that season, and we won a lot more games than they did. We secured the three seed, and they had the six seed, which led to the matchup in the first round. It was the first year the Bulls decided to wear black socks and black shoes, and it gave them this special mojo. It's not that Michael needed the extra help, but it seemed to make his teammates play better. We had played poorly in Game Four and should have lost that ballgame, but Jordan missed two free throws. It allowed us to take that game in overtime and win. It gave Jordan some added fuel as we headed back home for the fifth and final game. We were such competitive teams, and it led to some great games between us.*

Ehlo goes into further detail on what happened with "the shot":

We had a simple "give and go" play moments before with me and Larry Nance that led to me hitting the go-ahead shot to put us up by one point with seconds to go. The play worked to perfection as all five of us on the court did our job to execute it. The problem was that it left three seconds for the greatest player of our lifetime. To tell you the truth, we did something that we never did before. Coach Wilkens was one of those coaches that kept someone on the vision of the ball, for some reason, he chose to pull Nance off that assignment and called for a double team on Jordan. I think if I had been playing one-on-one with him, I would have played him harder. But because I had the help, I may have slacked off a little bit. When Jordan juked Larry on the first move, I ran over to catch him, and by the time I got there Jordan was already coming back the other way, so I went flying across him like E.T. across the moon and went right by him. I kept my hand in his face as long as I could, but he had the ability to stop on a dime, pull up and hit the shot. When I watched it go in, it was the agony of defeat. Those three seconds seemed like slow motion to watch him get that shot off and make that play. When you talk to Michael or anyone who was with the Bulls at that time, they will all say that shot was exactly what propelled them into their championships.

The following season, 1989–90, would be known for some critical injuries to Daugherty and Nance, as well as a controversial trade. Wayne Embry took a major chance that never panned out when he traded away young phenomenon Ron Harper. On November 16, 1989, the Cavs traded Ron Harper and three future draft picks to the Los Angeles Clippers for Danny Ferry and Reggie Williams. It was a calculated risk based on of the large amount of hype surrounding Danny Ferry's amateur career. It ended up being one of the worst trades in Cleveland Cavs history and one that is still discussed today.

Danny Ferry had gone to Duke University after being considered one of the best high school athletes in America. From DeMatha Catholic High School in Maryland, he was voted *Parade Magazine*'s "Prep Player of the Year." Since Ferry played so well during his college basketball career, many considered him to be the next Larry Bird. He was a two-time ACC Player of the Year, a member of the 1989 NCAA All-American first team and the 1989 USPI College Player of the Year. Later that year, he was drafted by the Los Angeles Clippers as the second overall pick in the draft. However,

Ferry had no interest in playing for the Clippers. Instead, he chose to play in Europe for the Italian League. He continued to excel while playing in Europe, averaging twenty-three points a game. The Clippers eventually grew tired of waiting for Ferry to come home to play for them, so they traded his rights to the Cavs. Once Ferry agreed to play for Cleveland, Embry signed him a to a ten-year contract. Sadly for Cleveland fans everywhere, Ferry would go down as one of the biggest NBA busts of all time, as he never lived up to his expectations. He averaged double digits in scoring only twice in his entire NBA career.

However, the Cavs did manage to make the playoffs that year despite the injuries. They finished with a 42-40 record, good enough for fourth place in the Eastern Conference Central Division. They ran into Charles Barkley and the Philadelphia 76ers in the first round of the playoffs, and Sir Charles and his teammates eliminated the Cavs in five hard-fought games.

The 1990–91 season got off to a horrible start as the Cavs did not have their full complement of draft picks due to the Danny Ferry trade. Things went from bad to worse as all-star point guard Mark Price suffered multiple injuries and appeared in only sixteen games all season. Power forward John "Hot Rod" Williams suffered season-long injuries as well, and the Cavs finished with their worst record in years at 33-49. The injury to Price and the poor results that followed further proved how crucial it is to have a good point guard to keep everything moving smoothly on the floor.

The 1991–92 season would be remembered as one of the best in Cavs history. It was a perfect mix of players in their prime, young players improving daily and veterans playing with the energy of rookies, all blended together with a Hall of Fame head coach. With a full roster all season and their confidence growing daily, the Cavs cruised to an impressive 57-25 record. They finished in second place in the Eastern Conference Central Division with high hopes of going far into the playoffs. Basketball fever had returned to Cleveland, as the Cavs had the fans clamoring for a rematch with the vaunted Chicago Bulls.

The Cavs promptly disposed of Drazen Petrovic, Derrick Coleman and the rest of the New Jersey Nets in the first round of the playoffs, earning a matchup with the perennial playoff contenders, the Boston Celtics. The matchup with Boston proved to be a classic as it was a back-and-forth battle that went all seven games. Early on, the Cavs fell behind in the series 2–1. Then, the pivotal Game Four went to overtime at the Boston Garden. Behind a thirty-two-point performance from Larry Nance, the Cavs left Boston with the win. Game Five at the Richfield Coliseum was a tight one throughout the first half, as neither team could pull away. The Cavs, behind the halftime adjustments from Wilkens, came out in the second half with guns blazing. They outscored the Celtics by eleven in the third quarter and never looked back, winning the game and taking a 3–2 lead in the series. Craig Ehlo describes how it felt to advance so far so quickly in the playoffs after early exits in previous years:

> *The final game of Larry Bird's career was in the old Richfield Coliseum, and it was very loud. It was a rough go for me because I had torn my MCL about six weeks prior. So when we got into the playoffs, I was still reeling and had to guard Petrovic in the first round. Then, in the second round, I had to guard Reggie Lewis, who had been averaging 35 points a game against us. In the finals, we had to face Chicago again, and even with Gerald Wilkins it was a nightmare. I thought we had finally reached the pinnacle of all those years that we had put together before losing in six games to the Bulls.*

Unfortunately, after a great fifth game, many Cleveland fans would like to forget Game Six, as the Cavs got crushed 122–91. Larry Nance reflects on reaching the Eastern Conference championship by beating Boston and the overall atmosphere in the Coliseum that day:

> *Derrick Coleman wore me out in the first round—he was very tough. Then, it was incredible to beat Boston with it being Larry Bird's last ride. I thought that if another team played together as well as we did, it was Boston because they really did play as a team. That series was two great teams out there playing great team ball, which made it very enjoyable. Then we ran into "the man" again.*

A loud crowd packed the Richfield Coliseum on May 17, 1992, to see the final game of the exciting series. The Cavs ended Larry Bird's Hall of Fame career on a sour note as they defeated his Celtics 122–104. Just like many times that season, the win was a total team effort, with all five starters scoring in the double digits. John "Hot Rod" Williams, who was coming off the bench in that series, managed to score twenty points. The Cavs were off to the Eastern Conference championship round for the first time since the "miracle season."

Waiting for the Cavs in the 1992 Eastern Conference championship round was their old friend Michael Jordan and his Chicago Bulls. The Cavs managed to make the series interesting by winning a couple games, but in the end, the developing dynasty of the Bulls was too much to overcome.

The following season, the Cavs would reach the playoffs yet again, this time making it to the second round before getting swept by Chicago. The addition of superstar Gerald Wilkens from the New York Knicks proved to be helpful but still not enough to get past the Bulls. Sadly, that series marked the last Wilkens would spend in Cleveland as head coach. The Cavs made the decision after the playoffs to go with Mike Fratello, a former Atlanta Hawks coach turned analyst. It was a move that brought to a close one of the brightest eras in Cleveland basketball history.

Lenny Wilkens went on to become one of the greatest coaches of all time, later coaching in Atlanta, Toronto and New York before retiring from the bench in 2005. By the time his career was over, he was inducted into the Hall of Fame again, this time as a coach. He won 1,332 games as a head coach. By the time he retired from active coaching, he had the most wins in NBA coaching history (Don Nelson later broke that record in 2010). In 1996, the NBA voted Wilkens as one of its all-time ten greatest coaches. Craig Ehlo also shares his admiration of Coach Wilkens:

> *It was unbelievable because I had watched him with his Sonics teams. He had a mild-mannered disposition, but he had a "rip your heart out" competitiveness in him as well. You may not see it in his body language, but that was the way he played and coached. I loved that, and that's exactly what I wanted to be like. I remember I rode with him on the plane the first day I got there, and he was trying to explain to me some of the offensive things we were going to try to do. I remember after that the game when I didn't play, he called me in and told me I would play the next night, which was a great thing because he really took me under his wing. He made me feel wanted and needed, and it was all because of him having that kind of demeanor. He loved us no matter what because it was a hardworking town and a hardworking team. The people of Cleveland still loved us no matter what happened.*

Larry Nance wrapped up his playing career after the 1994 season, retiring as a Cavalier. The Cavs decided to retire his number twenty-two jersey, which now proudly hangs in the rafters at Quicken Loans Arena. Larry finished his career as a three-time all-star and was known for being one of the best shot blockers of all time. While playing in Cleveland, Nance was voted to the All-Defensive team once and the All-Defensive second team twice. Nance describes his ability to play defense and shot block:

Those are the stats I love because I consider those to be effort stats. I learned how to block shots from my uncle, who told me that since most people are right-handed, if I learned how to block shots with my left hand, it would keep me out of foul trouble. I had a god-given ability to be able to jump, and I loved blocking shots because it was a definitive positive and a sign of hard work. It was something I loved to do, and a lot of times once you start blocking shots, the other team will start looking to avoid shooting on you—then you know you have them. As long as what I do on the court can help my team win, I'm all about that stat. It is the only one that matters.

Nance also discloses how it feels to have his jersey number retired and to be able to spend time with his family:

It feels great because this organization is filled with classy people and great owners. I think the owner now makes it a great place to be. I still live in Akron, Ohio, the same place I lived when I played here, because I love the fans, not the weather. Right now, I have a son in Wyoming, a daughter who just graduated from Dayton and a thirteen-year-old son who lives with us. I spend a lot of time with them. I'm close to opening up my own basketball facility down in Akron to teach basketball to kids. I want to teach these kids old-school basketball, how to play the game the right way. I would love to have my hands in racing, but it is so expensive and I can't do it without sponsors. I still love racing just as much as I always have.

Brad Daugherty would be celebrated as one of the greatest players in Cavaliers history. By the time his career ended in 1994, he had five All-Star Game appearances. He averaged nearly twenty points a game and, to that point, was the all-time leading scorer and rebounder for the Cavs. He went on to hold both of those records for several years. His jersey number, forty-three, also proudly hangs in the rafters of Quicken Loans arena. His career could have reached even greater heights if he hadn't been forced to retire at the age of twenty-eight because of chronic back injuries. Larry Nance, who was often in awe of his teammate Daugherty, recalls:

Brad was very skilled and didn't beat his chest, but he killed the best in the league on a nightly basis. He was also the best passing center and had a true understanding for the game. He could score and rebound with the best of them.

Mark Price is widely considered the most popular player to ever wear a Cleveland Cavaliers uniform. He seemed to be good at everything he did on the court, and the fans loved him for it. He knew how to score, how to pass and how to shoot free throws with a precision seldom seen before. He left the Cavs after the 1995 season and spent a few more years in the league before retiring. He would be remembered as one of the league's most consistent shooters, finishing with an incredible 90 percent free throw percentage and a 40 percent rate from beyond the three-point arc. His retired jersey also hangs proudly in the rafters of Quicken Loans Arena. Larry Nance notes that Mark Price was a "great, smart, energetic point guard who made everything easy for his teammates around him. He just knew how to play ball!"

Craig Ehlo followed Lenny Wilkens to the Atlanta Hawks for a couple years before ending his career in Seattle as a Supersonic. Nearly thirty years after his time in Cleveland, Ehlo is still seen as one of the most beloved figures in Cleveland sports history. He had a solid career and was respected by his teammates and fans because of his work ethic and approach. Larry notes that Ehlo was "a hard worker who came to play hard every game and always gave 100 percent. He always had to guard the toughest guys, and that was OK with him because he wanted to."

Ehlo has also had a few chances to meet Michael Jordan since he has retired. He describes one of those experiences:

> I took my son down to Santa Barbara to Jordan's camp he runs for kids. On the last day, he signs autographs for everyone and they put him in the middle of a room. When my son came through there, he asked Jordan to sign his shoe. When Michael asked who he was, my son said, "I'm Austin Ehlo." And then Jordan called him in closer. He told my son that I had hit the shot to put the Cavs up before "the shot" took place right after that. I thought that was pretty cool of him to do that.

Ehlo has led a happy and busy life since retiring from the game. He notes

> I was lucky that after basketball, after I retired, I was able to get into broadcasting with the Seattle Sonics television. I got to announce with Kevin Calabro, who was one of the best play-by-play guys in the business. I did that for two years before arriving in Spokane, where I started broadcasting Gonzaga basketball for the next seven years. I was able to work with Fox also doing PAC 10 games. I coached high school for a couple years after

that because I love being around the game, and as a broadcaster you don't have ownership in wins and losses. Sometimes after broadcasting a game, you would go home feeling vacant because of that fact. Now I'm 51 years old with a 24-year-old daughter that just graduated from college—that is something I never thought I would hear myself say. I have a 21-year-old who is playing football for Eastern Washington. I am currently coaching as an assistant football coach here with Eastern Washington. I spend my days in the gym as well as having a sophomore in high school. He is a football player, too. I grew up in Texas, so we have a love for football in our family as well. I come to work happy because I'm in shorts and a tank top, which is something that I did my whole life.

Ron Harper went on to have a stellar career. After suffering some injuries with the Clippers, he found his way to the Chicago Bulls and never looked back. He won three championships while playing with the Bulls and won two more playing with the Lakers before retiring in 2001. The Danny Ferry trade never quite panned out for Wayne Embry and the Cavs. However, Danny Ferry went on to become the general manager of the Cavaliers a few years after his playing days came to an end in 2003. This era of the Cavaliers remains the most beloved in franchise history, and for good reason!

Chapter 5

The Czar

The Cavaliers would enter the 1993–94 season with a new man in charge, as Mike Fratello was lured out of the broadcast booth and back onto the sidelines. Fratello was respected around the league from his time coaching in Atlanta, where he had led the Hawks to the playoffs five times in eight seasons during the 1980s. He spent the first half of the '90s on television calling games with Marv Albert for NBC. As a fan of his broadcasting, I was upset to see him leave the booth but excited to see what he could do with our hometown team. He would have to impress early and often because he was replacing a legend in Wilkens.

The 1993–94 season would also be the last played at the Richfield Coliseum. Starting the following season, the Cavaliers would be playing in their new home located in the heart of downtown Cleveland, the brand-new Gund Arena. They wanted to make their last season in Richfield memorable and hoped Fratello would be the fresh energy needed to lead them to a title. Michael Jordan had retired, and this was seen as the season that the Cavaliers might finally reach the pinnacle.

Once again, the team fought the injury bug as both Larry Nance and Brad Daugherty missed a large amount of time. This caused key reserves Terrell Brandon, Bobby Phills and rookie Chris Mills to step up their game as they saw increased minutes in the rotation. The combination of Mills, Tyrone Hill and Phills proved to be a staple the Cavaliers would count on for the next several seasons. Some fans joked that the combination of Hill, Mills and Phills sounded more like a law firm than a basketball team.

Tyrone Hill gets set to rebound. *Photo by Sheryl Scanlon.*

Whatever the "case" may be, Cleveland fans were just happy to see such young talent emerge.

At first, it looked like the coaching change was a mistake as the Cavs, thanks in part to injury issues, seemed to struggle with Fratello's new slow-paced offense. By mid-December, they were a season-low seven games below .500 as their record stood at 7-14. Fratello continued to push forward, and eventually the team found its stride and began to win. It took longer than they hoped, but by February 2, the Cavs had managed a winning record at 22-21. It was important that the Cavs finally pushed past the .500 mark, as the coaching change from Wilkens to Fratello was a big enough one that they did not want more fans and media questioning the move.

Once the Cavaliers surpassed the .500 mark, they never looked back and kept on winning. They went on an eleven-game winning streak and once again had everyone in Cleveland talking Cavs basketball. They finished the season at 47-35, a record good enough for the sixth seed in the highly talented Eastern Conference and a rematch with the rival Chicago Bulls. The Cavaliers were seen as a legitimate threat to possibly knock off the three-time defending NBA champions.

Hopes were high that the Cavaliers could upset the Bulls that season because it would be the first time Michael Jordan was not on the playoff roster.

Mike Fratello gets ready to lead the Cavs onto the court. *Photo by Sheryl Scanlon.*

Jordan had temporarily retired to try his hand at major-league baseball with the Chicago White Sox. Despite the lack of "His Airness," the Bulls were still very talented and managed to sweep the Cavaliers in three games.

Bobby Phills, Danny Ferry and Terrell Brandon exit the court after a win. *Photo by Sheryl Scanlon.*

The new-look Cavs under Mike Fratello. *Photo by Sheryl Scanlon.*

The Gund Arena would open in time for the beginning of the 1994–95 season. It was a key piece in the new gateway plaza that included the beautiful Jacobs Field. The arena was named after Gordon Gund and would go on to host every major sporting event the city could offer, including several WWF pay-per-views and *Monday Night Raw* and *Smackdown* episodes. This included Survivor Series 2004 and Summerslam 1996. It also hosted the circus, monster truck rallies, Disney on Ice, musical performances by the industry's top stars and even a visit by President Bill Clinton. The crowning jewel was the 1997 All-Star Game, which featured a ceremony honoring the NBA's fifty greatest players. The Gund was the new place to be, and the Cavaliers were sure to deliver.

The Cavs brought in veteran free-agent big man Michael Cage to help in the frontcourt. They would need the added size, as Brad Daugherty and Larry Nance had both retired. Mark Price was also winding down his time as the point guard in Cleveland, getting ready to hand over the reins to Terrell Brandon. Second-year forward Chris Mills continued to step up and led the team in scoring. Tyrone Hill continued to do his part and was second on the team in scoring while also leading the team in rebounds. Bobby Phills, who was once an end-of-the-bench player, showed how far he had come by finishing second on the team in assists and in the top five in scoring.

The Cavaliers stayed around the .500 mark for the entire season before finishing with a record of 43-39. They then had to face the defending Eastern Conference champion New York Knicks in the first round of the playoffs. The Knicks were led by all-stars such as Patrick Ewing, Charles Oakley and John Starks and directed by coaching legend Pat Riley. The loaded Knicks team would prove to be too much for the Cavaliers to handle, as they disposed of the Cavs in four games before being knocked out by Reggie Miller and the Indiana Pacers in the next round.

The Cavaliers had made the playoffs in each of Mike Fratello's first two seasons, and they looked to make it a three-peat as they entered the 1995–96 season. They traded aging veteran Mark Price to the Golden State Warriors for a draft pick to be used at a later time. They also traded "Hot Rod" Williams for veteran sharpshooter Dan Majerle. Many felt the team would be a threat all season.

The Cavaliers immediately had everyone second-guessing their high hopes as they started the season with seven straight losses. It was stunning, as the Fratello-led team was far more talented than its record would indicate. They eventually got hot, however, and were able to right the ship. They went 15-5 in their next twenty games to reach 20-17 as they neared the All-Star Break.

The Cavaliers remained hot in the second half of the season, which was highlighted by an eight-game winning streak in February. They also had several three-game winning streaks in both March and April. The Cavs finished with a 47-35 record, which was good enough for the fourth overall seed in the Eastern Conference. They would have a rematch with the New York Knicks waiting for them. This time, however, the Cavaliers would have the home court advantage.

Mike Fratello and the Cavaliers continued to face first-round struggles as, despite having the home court advantage, they failed to win a single game in the series. The Knicks swept the Cavaliers right out of the playoffs for the second

Terrell Brandon (11) took over point guard duties from Mark Price. *Photo by Sheryl Scanlon.*

straight season. It was a disappointing end to a promising season. The Knicks were vulnerable that season, but the Cavs failed to capitalize.

But there were some bright spots for the Cavs. Terrell Brandon continued to excel as the leader of the team by scoring 19.3 points a game. He also led the team in assists, with 6.5 a game. Chris Mills was a solid scoring threat as well, averaging 15.0 points a game to go along with Bobby Phills and his 14.6 points a contest. Dan Majerle did not pan out as the 3-point shooting threat they hoped he would be, as he averaged only one 3-pointer per game. Despite the lack of offense from Majerle, however, the Cavs managed to score plenty of points that season.

With three members of the backcourt showing such promising talent, the Cavaliers' front office focused on the frontcourt in the draft that June. They owned the twelfth and twentieth picks in the first round. With the twelfth pick, they took Vitaly Potapenko, who was never anything more than average during his entire NBA career. Their second pick in the first round, however, turned out to be one of the greatest players to ever put on a Cavaliers jersey.

With the twentieth pick in the 1996 NBA draft, the Cleveland Cavaliers selected Zydrunas Ilgauskas from Lithuania. Due to foot surgery, he wouldn't be able to play until his second NBA season. However, the Cavaliers felt he was worth the risk.

The Cavs got off to a hot start and jumped out to an 11-5 record. They kept their momentum in December and rolled off five straight wins at one point. On January 4, 1997, they reached a season-high eleven games over .500 with a record of 21-10. With the All-Star Game headed to the Gund Arena that season, Terrell Brandon was having an all-star season. It seemed as though the stars were aligning perfectly for Fratello and the Cavs.

The momentum came to a streaking halt as the Cavs hit a rough patch in mid-January by losing six straight games. They bounced back before hitting several more skids and slowly but surely played themselves out of a playoff spot. They finished with a surprising 42-40 record, including a season-ending loss to the Washington Bullets. It was a second-half collapse that few saw coming, and it would signal major changes ahead. The Cavaliers were about to take on a very different look, complete with a Reign Man and some young guns!

Chapter 6

The Young Guns

Heading into the 1997–98 season, the Cavaliers were ready to start making some major moves. The previous year had been the first of many in which they didn't make the playoffs, and they were not ready to repeat that fact in their second season in their beautiful new home. The Cavaliers' ownership group and general manager Wayne Embry were committed to positive change. They were stocked up with draft picks in the upcoming 1997 NBA draft, and they determined to make each one count. Embry had used draft picks and trades once before to change the luck of the Cavs, and he was determined to pull it off again. Gone were all the aging veterans; instead, he had plenty of options to start creating a team Fratello could once again mold into a winner.

The NBA draft was loaded that year with such future all-stars as Tim Duncan, Keith Van Horn, Chauncey Billups and Tracy McGrady. The Cavs were the proud owners of the thirteenth and sixteenth picks in the first round. They were in prime position to infuse the aging lineup with some much-needed youth, and this new group of college phenoms could only help that effort.

With the thirteenth pick, they selected Derek Anderson, a senior shooting guard out of the University of Kentucky. Anderson was on UK's 1996 NCAA national championship team, a roster that featured nine eventual NBA players. He was not only talented on the court but also possessed sharp mental skills, graduating with a pharmacy degree. A good shooter who hustled on defense, he would provide a solid number-two guard when needed, and he also had the talent to start right away. He was even a great bowler, as was shown in his draft video, which my brother Don and I watched at the Quicken Loans Arena the night of the draft. It showed that he was skilled in multiple areas and possessed the talent to play several positions in Fratello's lineup. The only concern with Anderson was that he was coming off a torn ACL in college. Torn ACLs are common injuries but can shorten a player's career if not treated and rehabbed correctly.

Zydrunas Ilgauskas's number eleven now hangs in the rafters of Quicken Loans Arena. *Photo by Betty Cantley.*

With the sixteenth pick, the Cavaliers selected Brevin Knight, a point guard out of Stanford University. Knight was seen as a solid pick and a suitable backup for current starter Terrell Brandon. No one knew it at the time, but the need for a good starting point guard would suddenly become urgent only a short time later. Knight had a productive college career at Stanford, where he is the all-time leader in assists (780) and steals (298) and third all-time in scoring (1,714). The Cavaliers getting him that late in the first round was seen as a steal.

The Cavaliers owned one more pick in the draft, the forty-fourth overall pick. They took Cedric Henderson with their final selection. Henderson was a six-foot, seven-inch small forward who had size and speed and had been outstanding during his career at the University of Memphis. All three picks were seen as suitable backups but also talents who could step in if an injury were to occur to any of the current starters. GM Wayne Embry and the Cavaliers' front office had different plans.

On September 25, 1997, Wayne Embry pulled the trigger on a blockbuster deal that no one in the NBA saw coming. He sent all-star point guard Terrell Brandon and veteran starting power forward Tyrone Hill to the Milwaukee Bucks for Sherman Douglass. However, it was part of a three-team trade

Sportswriter Vince McKee with Cavs play-by-plan man Fred McLeod. *Courtesy of www. vpeterpress.com.*

The young guns kept the arena on fire. *Courtesy of www.vpeterpress.com.*

that saw Vin Baker leave the Bucks for the Sonics and Seattle send all-star Shawn Kemp to the Cavaliers.

It was a major deal, as Kemp was seen as one of the best players in the game. He had also led the Sonics to the NBA Finals only two years prior. His jersey was one of the highest-selling ones in the league, showing exactly how popular the young all-star truly was. He was the most popular player and one of the best ones to ever wear a Seattle Supersonic uniform.

While playing at Concord High School in Indiana, Kemp was seen as one of the best high school players in the country. By the time he finished his high school career, he held the school's all-time scoring record. In fact, he broke every scoring record the school had to offer. So impressive was Kemp that the University of Kentucky offered him a full scholarship to come play for it. The problem was that Kemp scored horribly on the SAT and was not eligible to play in his freshman year. Because of his issues at Kentucky, he transferred to Trinity Valley Community College in Texas. After a semester at TVCC, where he did not play, nineteen-year-old Shawn Kemp decided to enter the NBA draft. It was a bold move and one that was rarely made at the time. While playing with the Sonics, Kemp improved drastically and became a five-time all-star.

But Wayne Embry was not done dealing yet; a week later, he brought in sharp-shooting Wesley Person from the Phoenix Suns. It was another major coup for the Cavaliers to pull off because Person was such a vital threat from anywhere beyond the arc. The Cavs had completely reshaped their starting lineup in only a few months. With a healthy Zydrunas Ilgauskas ready to take his place in the middle, their second season in their new home would be a memorable one, with Fratello ready to lead his young guns to countless victories and a playoff push!

It took a little time for the young team to mesh, as the Cavs lost their first two games as well as six of their first ten. Mike Fratello kept them working hard, however, and they managed to get hot by winning ten straight games. Six of the ten wins came on the road as they knocked off Philadelphia, Charlotte, Minnesota, Golden State, Vancouver and even the Los Angeles Lakers, all in their own buildings. They treated the fans to four wins at home during that stretch as well, including wins against Washington, Boston, Denver and Phoenix. They were beating a who's who of NBA powerhouses and quickly becoming a force to reckon with.

They remained hot and were 25-16 at the halfway point of the season. It was a surprising record for a team with four rookie starters. They were playing incredibly well together with the veteran leadership of Shawn

Kemp, who continued to perform as one of the top power forwards in the league. One concern was that the Cavs were 0-3 in overtime games at that point, and many believed that their youth and stamina might be hurting them. They needed to start performing better when the extra frame came along. It was a great test for the young bunch, in terms of both endurance and heart.

As they entered mid-March, they got hot once again and rattled off winning streaks of four and five games, including overtime wins against the New York Knicks and Detroit Pistons. It was a positive sign as the young team was starting to take shape and peak at a crucial time in the season. Shawn Kemp was continuing to play at an all-star level, while the young guns improved with each game. The Cavaliers were starting to be seen as a real threat as the playoffs neared.

The Cavaliers finished with a 47-35 record that season. It was unheard of for a team that started four rookies to have a winning record twelve games over .500. The fans were ecstatic as their Cavs were about to enter the Eastern Conference playoffs to take on the Indiana Pacers. Shawn Kemp finished as the team's leading scorer, averaging 18.0 points a game. Wesley Person continued to be a sharp shooter off the bench as he led the team in 3-pointers. Ilgauskas averaged 13.9 points a game with 8.8 rebounds. Derek Anderson also chipped in with a double-digit scoring average as he put up 11.7 points a game. Second-round rookie sensation Cedric Henderson helped out with 10.1 points a contest as well. Rookie point guard Brevin Knight did an amazing job finding the open man as he led the team in assists with an average of 8.2 a game.

Mary Schmitt Boyer, who has been the Cavs beat reporter for the *Cleveland Plain Dealer* for nearly twenty years, had these comments to share about the young team:

> *Everyone thought that this was going to be to the beginning of quite the era for the Cavs. It didn't work out because of the injuries to both Z and Anderson. I believe they succeeded in spite of Shawn, who may have left his better years behind him in Seattle.*

Heading into the playoffs, the Cavaliers were firing on all cylinders, and they would have to be, as the Indiana Pacers were a solid team in their own right. The Pacers came into the first round matchup as a heavy favorite against the young Cavaliers. The Pacers had finished the regular season with an impressive fifty-eight wins behind the incredible shooting of guard

Reggie Miller. The core of the Pacer team had been playing together for many years, and this looked like it might be their best chance to reach the finals. Point guard Mark Jackson had no issues finding Reggie Miller open on the perimeter for countless three-pointers.

The Cavaliers were the sixth seed, so they had to begin the best-of-five-game series in Indiana against the third-seeded Pacers. The Cavaliers dug themselves an early hole in the game and could not get out. Despite double-digit scoring nights from Ilgauskas, Anderson and Kemp, with twenty-five, the Cavaliers simply could not hang around with the powerful Indiana Pacer team. Veteran Chris Mullin had twenty points for the Pacers, while Miller contributed with nineteen. Rik Smits and Dale Davis both had double-digit scoring nights as well, and Mark Jackson dished out ten assists in the 106–77 blowout. The Pacers possessed the complete package needed to win at a high level.

Down one game heading into Game Two of the series, the Cavaliers knew it was vital to win at least one game in Indiana so they wouldn't have to face a giant deficit heading back home. They managed to make it a little closer but still fell short in the end by a score of 92–86. Shawn Kemp once again led the Cavaliers with twenty-seven points, but it was not enough. Ilgauskas chipped in with twenty-five points, but the rest of the team was ice cold all night. The Pacers had four starters and two players off the bench score in the double digits, and they now had a 2–0 stranglehold heading back to Cleveland for Game Three.

Game Three was the first playoff game to be held at Gund Arena. The Mike Fratello–led squad was on a mission to play better defense and avoid getting swept. They did just that as they held Miller in check all night and limited him to only eighteen points. Shawn Kemp, who was on a mission to keep the series and the season alive, once again led the Cavaliers with thirty-one points as Brevin Knight continued to do his part by dishing out five assists and swiping three steals. Derek Anderson also had a great game, scoring eleven points while collecting five rebounds and dishing out five assists. The Cavaliers had managed to stave off elimination and force a pivotal Game Four. I remember going to that game with my brother Don, as he was able to get tickets off of a scalper at the last second. It was awesome and a memory I will always cherish.

All good things eventually come to an end, and they did for the Cavaliers on April 30, 1998, as they dropped Game Four to the Indiana Pacers by a score of 80–74. They fought hard all night and led for several moments before finally running out of gas in the end. A couple damaging Reggie

Miller three-pointers spelled doom for the young Cavaliers team as they could never seem to pull ahead for good. Shawn Kemp had twenty-one points, and Derek Anderson chipped in with an impressive eighteen, but it was too little too late. The Cavaliers had fought hard all season but came up just a bit short in the end.

They had nothing to be ashamed of, as a team with four rookies playing so many minutes to win so many games was simply unheard of. With the young, talented roster in place and the savvy veteran coach leading them, one thing was for sure: good times were ahead for the die-hard basketball fans of Cleveland, and there didn't appear to be anything that could screw it up. Little did anyone know that a major strike was on the horizon, and it would be quite some time before the players saw the court again. It was a strike that could have been easily avoided, but as usual, money does all the talking.

Chapter 7

The Strike

Just when it seemed that playoff basketball would be returning to Cleveland for good, the players' strike hit and caused the beginning of the 1998–99 season to be delayed. It robbed most of the momentum the Cavaliers franchise had managed to build the previous season. The Cavs had all five starters set to return and were expected to be a force once again in the Eastern Conference Central Division. The problem was that by the time the strike ended and the season began on February 5, 1999, Shawn Kemp, who was not used to having that much time off between seasons, had put on serious weight.

The once stealthy Kemp was now slow; he wasn't even close to the talented player from seasons before. He had finished the previous season at 254 pounds, but when he reported to camp, he weighed in at 280. (It was later revealed in Wayne Embry's autobiography that Kemp actually reported in at 315 pounds.) Kemp would have to force himself to get back in shape quickly because the season, which had been cut short, would last only fifty games. When Fratello asked Kemp why he let himself get out of shape, he said, "Coach, I didn't think we were coming back." Wayne Embry went on to further detail what exactly went wrong and the steps the Cavaliers took to fix the problem:

> *Whatever teams were in the best shape would definitely have an advantage in the short schedule. We were not one of them. We were all disappointed in Shawn's physical condition. With the money we were paying him,*

The strike kept arenas empty. *Photo by Sam Bourquin.*

we had every reason to expect him to stay in shape. It was not as if he could not afford to hire people to help him do that. The Cleveland Clinic nutritionist put him on a diet, but Shawn did not have the discipline to adhere to it. We even offered to have a chef go to his house and prepare meals for him. I told Shawn the same thing I told Mel Turpin years ago: "I don't want anyone playing for me that weighs more than me." That did not work either.

The fact that an athlete of Kemp's caliber showed such gluttony and laziness came as a shock to many, but it would become an all too familiar trend all around sports in the coming years. Several players would rest on their laurels once the big contract was signed. Kemp was just the latest example of an athlete who once had it all and let it get away from him. It wasn't too much longer after that season that Kemp ate himself right out of the league, as other teams were unwilling to take a chance on his act.

With the reduced schedule, a fast start would be a must for any chance at competing for a playoff spot. The Cavaliers failed to do that as they dropped their first three games to start the campaign. Losses at Atlanta and Boston were coupled with a home-opening loss to Indiana. The Cavs were able to rebound from the slow start with a five-game winning streak, rattling off wins against Charlotte, San Antonio, Orlando, New York and New Jersey. It gave fans and media the false hope that the club might still be a serious threat to go deep into the playoffs. Sadly for fans and players alike, the Cavs went on to lose their next four consecutive games and close out the opening month with a 5-7 record. They managed to stay right around the .500 mark as they finished March with a 14-14 record. They kept things steady but couldn't seem to get hot and stay hot long enough to make a difference.

They finally started to catch fire in early April by achieving two three-game winning streaks. It was looking good until the inevitable happened—they started to run out of gas, much like everyone feared they would. Because of the poor conditioning issues, the Cavs were unable to compete late in games and lost seven straight down the stretch. They won only one of their final eleven games and finished with a 22-28 record. It was a huge disappointment for everyone involved. When the season ended in May, they could only blame themselves and think of what could have been had they stayed in better shape during the off-season. If they had better endurance and more veteran leadership instead of the out-of-shape Kemp, they could have held on to a playoff spot.

Shawn Kemp once again led the team in scoring with twenty-plus points a game. His main help down low, however, was hurt before they could really get things going. In what became a trend early in his career, Zydrunas Ilgauskas was hurt and played only five games because of a serious foot injury. Ilgauskas was loaded with potential, but the injury kept him off the court when the Cavaliers sorely needed him.

Their other big man, Vitaly Potapenko, was traded away midway through the season to the Boston Celtics for Andrew DeClercq and a first-round draft pick used on point guard Andre Miller. It turned out to be a great trade as Miller was very reliable and productive for several years to come. The outside shooting declined greatly, as no one on the team was seen as a real threat. Wesley Person managed to hit about one three-pointer a game, but that was the sole exception. Without their big men and no outside game, the strike-shortened season was just too much for them to overcome. Brevin Knight and Derek Anderson both tried their best but could not overcome the sophomore slumps.

The biggest effect from the losing season was the decision of Gordon Gund to fire Mike Fratello and Wayne Embry. Someone had to be the scapegoat, and with no playoff series wins in his coaching career in Cleveland, sadly,

Fratello was given the axe. His inability to get the Cavaliers out of the first round of the playoffs in any of their trips had not helped his cause. The Cavaliers had entered a state of transition—how long the rebuild would take and what it would entail was anyone's guess.

Chapter 8

The Dark Years

Randy Wittman was the next to step up and take on the challenge of head coach. Wittman was born in Indiana, which is the lifeblood of basketball in our country. He had an NBA pedigree as he played for nearly ten years in the league. He started his career with the Atlanta Hawks and spent five seasons with them. After leaving Atlanta, he spent time with the Sacramento Kings before finishing up his career where his love of basketball began, playing for the Indiana Pacers.

Wittman remained in Indiana after his playing days were over, becoming an assistant coach for the Pacers. Over the next several years, he also spent time with the coaching staffs of the Dallas Mavericks and Minnesota Timberwolves. While in Minnesota, he helped mold the career of young superstar Kevin Garnett. It was his excellent work with Garnett that got him noticed by Cleveland and also the rest of the league. Wittman had a young, talented roster, and if he could install his fast-paced offense, the Cavaliers would once again become a playoff threat.

Wittman would have a new point guard to lead the team, as GM Jim Paxson, to the surprise of many, took Andre Miller out of Utah with the eighth pick in the 1999 NBA draft. The draft was loaded with talent that year as it boasted perennial all-stars such as Elton Brand, Steve Francis, Baron Davis, Lamar Odom, Wally Szczerbiak, Richard Hamilton, Shawn Marion, Jason Terry, Ron Artest, Andrei Kirilenko, Manu Ginobili and several others. Miller would compete with incumbent point guard Brevin Knight. It turned out not to be much of a competition, however, as Miller was loaded with talent, and it didn't take long for the Cavaliers' front office to realize it.

Miller was coming off a stellar college career at Utah and looked poised to take the NBA by storm. While at Utah, he became a starting point guard in his freshman year and never looked back. His career peaked in his sophomore year, when he took the Utah Utes to the NCAA championship game. He gained national attention during the tournament despite the championship game loss to the Kentucky Wildcats. His senior season at Utah was filled with awards and milestones. He was voted the player of the year for the Western Athletic Conference. He was also voted to the conference first teams on both offense and defense. Miller built quite the name for himself while at Utah, and the pick was seen as a steal for Cleveland.

The Cavaliers also held the eleventh pick of the opening round and used it on Trajan Langdon out of Duke University. They hoped to have better luck with Langdon than they did with fellow Duke alumni Danny Ferry. Langdon grew up in Anchorage, Alaska, where he went on to play at East Anchorage High School. He performed well there, amassing over 2,200 career points and earning Alaskan player of the year honors on three separate occasions. While at Duke, he broke the team record for most three-pointers. His spot-on shooting earned him the nickname the "Alaskan Assassin." After graduating from Duke with degrees in mathematics and history, Langdon played for the U.S. National Team in the 1998 FIBA World Championship, where the United States won the bronze medal. Sadly for the Cavaliers, the success he had in college and internationally never carried over to his NBA career.

With the Cavaliers selecting two guards in the first round, it spelled the end for Derek Anderson in Cleveland. He was traded to the LA Clippers later that summer for small forward Lamond Murray, who was seen as a veteran presence and someone who wasn't afraid to take the big shot—or any shot, for that matter. Murray started off OK, but rumors quickly spread that he was more concerned about his jersey placement at the team shop than how many victories he was able to help his team achieve.

Wittman looked to run a very fast-paced offense. It appeared that his style was working as the Cavaliers got off to a strong start. A month and a half into the season, they held an 11-9 record, which was very respectable for a team in rebuilding mode. They were once again playing without starting center Zydrunas Ilgauskas, who was out for the entire season with another foot surgery. Since being drafted, it was the third season out of four in which a foot injury would keep Ilgauskas on the sidelines. It forced Wittman to play undersized and inexperienced centers in A.J. Bramlett, Andrew DeClercq and even Shawn Kemp. Behind the excellent play of rookie point guard Andre Miller and the sharp shooting of Wesley Person and Lamond Murray, the Cavaliers managed to run off two separate three-game winning streaks. They were playing well at home, winning nine of their first twelve. The good momentum would come to a screeching halt on December 15, 1999, with a lopsided loss to the New Jersey Nets on the road. The Cavaliers were unable to recover from the 111–101 loss, and it was the beginning of a seven-game losing streak. They managed to stop the bleeding with a win at home against the Washington Wizards before embarking on another rough patch of games that saw them go 5-11 in their next sixteen. They were suddenly 16-25, nine games under .500, and the season was disappearing fast. The month of February wasn't much better, as they endured losing streaks of five and six games apiece. March proved to be even worse, and by the time they reached April 1, they were stumbling to the finish with a 28-43 record. They managed to win four more games before the season ended, and the final tally was 32-50. It was a sad finish for a once proud franchise.

The main problem was a lack of team chemistry. Despite Miller showing solid ability to lead, Murray was unable to mesh with his other teammates, and it led to many lackluster nights on the hardwood. Langdon, who had been counted on to provide an offensive spark off the bench, failed to do so and averaged only 4.9 games, as injuries limited him to playing in only 10.0 games all season.

The house cleaning began shortly after the season ended as they traded away young shooting guard Bobby Sura. He was dealt to the Golden State Warriors as part of a three-team deal that saw J.R. Reid and Robert Traylor arrive from the Milwaukee Bucks. They also made a draft-day trade as they sent Jamal Crawford to Chicago for the Bulls' pick, center Chris Mihm. Both were very ill-fated moves on Paxson's part, as Traylor would struggle with weight issues and Crawford would go on to have a decent career.

They also looked to improve the bench with some veteran talent and proceeded to trade Andrew DeClercq to the Orlando Magic in exchange for veteran shooting guard Matt Harpring. A few weeks after the trade, they signed veteran backup point guard Bimbo Coles; his job would be to mentor young sensation Andre Miller. The summer ended with a trade that saw Shawn Kemp dealt to the Portland Trailblazers and Chris Gatling and Clarence Weatherspoon arrive from the Miami Heat. Gatling and Weatherspoon were both seen as veteran scoring threats who could really provide a nice boost both in the starting lineup and off the bench. The

Sportswriter Vince McKee with Martynas Andriuskevicius, who played in only six career games. *Courtesy of www.vpeterpress.com.*

Cavaliers were losing their best player in Kemp; however, the two-for-one deal was seen as a huge upgrade in the overall trade value.

The Cavaliers wasted no time in getting off to a red-hot start. They won their first four games, including a gutsy double-overtime win at home against the Sacramento Kings. They remained hot and held an impressive 15-7 record as they hit mid-December. The additions of Weatherspoon and Gatling were meshing well with sophomore sensation Andre Miller. It was at this point, however, that Zydrunas Ilgauskas once again went down with another season-ending foot injury. This proved to be a costly blow, as the Cavaliers couldn't recover from losing their biggest scoring and rebounding threat once again.

After the loss of Ilgauskas, the Cavaliers promptly went on a five-game losing streak. Things didn't get much better, and by midseason, the Cavs continued to struggle, holding a record of 20-22. The low point of the season was still to come, however, as they went on an eleven-game losing streak. Before the season was over, they would also endure two other seven-game losing streaks. They finished with the identical 32-50 record from the previous season. This would be the last year under the direction of head coach Randy Wittman, as he was let go shortly after the conclusion of the season.

Andre Miller had another strong season as he played in all eighty-two games and led the team in assists with an average of 8.3 per game. He also averaged 16.4 points a game while chipping in with 4-plus rebounds a game as well. Miller also continued to help his teammates improve, as new addition Chris Gatling led the team in scoring with 18.3 points a game. The loss of Zydrunas Ilgauskas proved to be too much to overcome as, at the time of his injury, the big man was averaging 14.4 points a game and almost 10.0 rebounds a game. No one on the roster was able to fill the void he left. Rookie center Chris Mihm did his best but averaged only 13.8 points a game and 8.6 rebounds a game. Mihm also played in only fifty-nine games due to injury issues. With Mihm and Ilgauskas out of the lineup, the Cavs were left without a dominant big man and could not compete.

With Wittman fired, it was once again up to Jim Paxson to find a suitable replacement to roam the sidelines. He hired two-time former NBA coach and former NBA player John Lucas. Lucas had been the head coach of the San Antonio Spurs from 1992 to 1994 but was let go after only two seasons. He then tried his luck in Philadelphia, where he coached the 76ers from 1994 to 1996 but had the same result. He had a poor record as a coach, and the move from Paxon to bring him in was another head-scratcher for fans and media.

Lucas had been an accomplished athlete before he got into coaching. An All-American at the University of Maryland, his college career was so impressive that he earned a spot on the U.S. National Team in the 1974 FIBA World Championships, where his team won a bronze metal. He was then selected as the first overall pick in the 1976 NBA draft by the Houston Rockets and went on to have a fine NBA career, even reaching the 1986 NBA Finals as a member of the Rockets. His story was also one of inspiration, as

Lucas had fought and overcome substance abuse addiction. He struggled with cocaine and alcohol before finally submitting himself into an NBA anti-drug and alcohol treatment center in order to clean up and also stay in the league. Lucas was successful in his fight against addiction and started programs of his own to help other athletes with rehabilitation. He used his own struggles to show others that their problems could be overcome if they sought the help they needed.

Lucas would need that positive attitude to turn around the Cavaliers' recent woes. With the major injury concerns of Zydrunas Ilgauskas still looming, the Cavs drafted another center, DeSagana Diop out of Senegal, with the eighth overall pick in the 2001 NBA draft. Diop never made it to college, as he played for Oak Hill Academy in Virginia, where he averaged 14.6 points, 13.2 rebounds and 8.1 blocks during his senior season. He led his team to a 33-0 record, which was good enough for a number-one national ranking. Diop was seen as a good replacement for Ilgauskas in case he never made it back to the full-time roster.

After drafting Diop, the Cavs made a deal to send Chris Gatling to the Miami Heat for shooting guard Ricky Davis. The three-team trade also saw power forward Brian Skinner arrive in Cleveland from Toronto. Davis was seen as a sharp shooter and someone who could generate points quickly. He had shown these abilities in his first three seasons in the league playing for both the Charlotte Hornets and Miami Heat. Davis stood six feet, seven inches and could play small forward as well as shooting guard. He wasn't seen as the greatest teammate or smartest player, however, and those faults would become quite evident only a short time after he arrived in Cleveland. (He once purposely missed a shot at the end of the game so he could try to secure the rebound and get his first career triple-double.) The deal was made right before the start of the season and didn't give his teammates much time to get used to his style of play.

The 2001–02 season did not get off to a good start as the Cavs lost six of their first seven games. After capturing a win on the road against Minnesota, they lost three straight to drop them to 2-9 on the season. It would be Lucas's task to get the team in order before the season was out of control. They managed to win four of five games in early December to bring their record to 9-12. However, that would be the closest they would get to a .500 record. They started the 2002 part of the campaign with a twelve-game losing streak. It was another bad stretch in a year that did not have many positives. They endured another six-game losing streak later in the season as well. Their final record was 29-53, which left plenty of room for improvement.

One bright spot was that center Zydrunas Ilgauskas had managed to play in sixty-two games before getting hurt once again and having to sit out the final twenty games of the season. He had started only twenty-three of those games and worked on a light schedule, as the Cavs wanted to ease him back into full-time play. It was crucial that his foot, as well as the rest of his body, could handle the wear and tear of a full NBA season.

Andre Miller once again stood out as the team leader. In just his third season, he led the team in both scoring and assists. Miller averaged 16.5 points, 10.9 assists and 4.7 rebounds a game. He was the brightest star in a Cavaliers uniform, and many fans thought he would be the key piece going forward during the rebuilding project.

Ricky Davis averaged 11.7 points a game in his first season in a Cavs uniform. The point production out of Davis was good; however, the rebounds and assists were both lacking. He averaged only 2.2 assists and three rebounds per game. Those were not impressive numbers for the shooting guard/small forward. His sole focus was scoring, not making the players around him better.

Trajan Langdon continued to fight the injury bug himself as he played in only forty-four games. His inability to stay healthy was a major concern, and some in the media had resorted to calling him "Tragic" Langdon because of the awful start to his career.

Heading into the off-season, many questions surrounded the upcoming season. Both fans and the media were talking about teams tanking the season to increase their draft positions for a shot at high school phenom LeBron James. With James being from the Akron area, he seemed like a perfect fit for the Cavs. But the fans thought it might be too good to be true.

The Cavaliers decided to ignore the LeBron hype for the time being and focus on the draft. They had the fifth overall pick and used it to select shooting guard Dajuan Wagner out of the University of Memphis. At six feet, two inches, Wagner was small for a shooting guard, and when combined with Andre Miller, the Cavaliers looked to have one of the shortest backcourts in all of basketball. But what Wagner lacked in size he made up for in heart and hustle. He once scored 100 points in a high school game and was never afraid to take the big shot. While playing at Camden High School in New Jersey, he averaged an amazing 42 points a game his senior season. By the end of his high school career, he had scored 3,462 points, the most by anyone to ever wear the Camden High jersey. He entered the NBA draft after only one year in college, and most scouts said he possessed many of the same skills as NBA superstar Allen Iverson.

The Cavaliers also landed a gem with their second-round pick out of Duke University, Carlos Boozer. A standout while playing in Chapel Hill, Boozer and his teammates had won the NCAA national championship in 2001. To get a player as highly touted as Boozer in the second round was seen as a major deal for the Cavaliers.

With Andre Miller running the point and being able to pass to sharp shooters such as Dajuan Wagner and Ricky Davis, the Cavaliers were suddenly an offensive threat. Combine that with the underneath presence of Carlos Boozer, and the Cavaliers seemed to be headed in the right direction. Everything seemed on pace for a turnaround season when, suddenly, a trade happened that no one saw coming.

On July 30, 2002, the Cavaliers traded away their best player, Andre Miller, and Bryant Stith to the Los Angeles Clippers for Harold Jamison and Darius Miles. The move was stunning because it left them without a starting point guard. They would later trade for Milt Palacio and sign free-agent point guard Smush Parker. However, neither Palacio nor Parker, or backup point guard Bimbo Coles, was capable of starting on a regular basis. The Cavs had a couple high-flying scorers in Miles and Davis, but without a point guard to get them the ball, it was looking like a very long season was ahead of them.

Some in the national media accused the Cavs of tanking the season so they could have a better chance at winning the draft lottery and thus winning the rights to pick LeBron James. Those conspiracy theorists had even more fuel to add to the fire when it was reported that James was allowed to participate in an off-season practice session with the team. It was unheard of to let a high school athlete practice with the pros, and it caused Lucas to get fined and suspended for the first two games of the upcoming 2002–03 season.

The Cavaliers opened up the season on the road against the Western Conference powerhouse Sacramento Kings. It was a blowout from the very first bounce of the ball. Sacramento exposed the Cavs' lack of firepower and ability to move the ball in a 94–67 blowout. Without a starting point guard, it didn't look like the Cavs would be improving anytime soon. It also didn't appear that they felt any urgency to get better via a trade or free-agent pickup. This only added more fuel to the tanking firestorm.

It wasn't too much longer after opening night that the Cavaliers started what would be a fifteen-game losing streak. By Christmas, their record was 6-24, with no improvement in sight. Things didn't get much better after that, and by the All-Star Break, John Lucas was fired as head coach. He left the team with an 8-34 record. In just over a season and a half as coach, Lucas had compiled a lowly thirty-seven wins. You couldn't put too much blame on the coach, however, as the franchise was going through some serious growing pains. Would the growing pains lead to the acquisition of the greatest high school player on the planet? Only time would tell.

Assistant coach Keith Smart took over for Lucas, but his luck wasn't much better, as the team finished the season tied with the Denver Nuggets for the worst record in the league at 17-65. The end of the season couldn't come soon enough for Cleveland and its fans, as the Cavs won two consecutive games only once the entire season.

The silver lining in the dark cloud was the fact that Zydrunas Ilgauskas played in eighty-one games. It was a great sign that he had fully recovered from years of foot injuries and surgeries. The play of "Z" was so impressive that he was voted onto the Eastern Conference All-Star team. He averaged 17.2 points a game along with 7.5 rebounds. He also led the team in blocks with 1.9 a night. If the Cavaliers were to improve, a healthy Zydrunas Ilgauskas would be crucial.

Also impressive was the play of rookie standout Carlos Boozer, who played in eighty-one games and averaged 10 points and 7.5 rebounds a game. Boozer, a second-round pick, was quickly looking like a major steal. He was also someone whom the Cavaliers knew they could count on to be their starting power forward for a long time to come, or so they thought. Boozer would eventually become one of the most hated men in the history of Cleveland sports.

One of the low points on the season was the play of recent first-round picks DeSagana Diop, Chris Mihm and Dajuan Wagner. Diop averaged a miserable 1.5 points a game with an almost invisible 2.7 rebounds per contest. Mihm wasn't too much better, as he averaged only 5.9 points a game and 4.4 rebounds. Dajuan Wagner looked solid at times but battled colitis issues and was able to play in only forty-seven games; however, he did average 13.4 points a game when he was able to suit up. The colitis ended up being the catalyst to his early exit from the league. His colitis was not amenable to medication, and a few years after being drafted, Wagner underwent surgery to remove his entire colon on October 25, 2005.

It was the Cavs' fifth straight season missing the playoffs, and they had gone through four head coaches in that time as well. This was very uncharacteristic for a Gordon Gund–owned team, and he looked for stability quickly. Luckily for Gund and the fans of Cleveland, the winds of change were blowing. A young king was set to arrive and take his throne.

Chapter 9
The King Arrives

The good thing about having such a horrible record was that it increased the Cavs' chances at winning the annual draft lottery. The NBA does not have a traditional-style draft, which allows teams to pick in order of record. Instead, it holds a draft lottery, which determines the first three picks in a random lotto fashion. On June 26, 2003, after five years of having bad luck, the Cavs finally turned their fate around when they won the NBA draft lottery. The reason why the number-one pick was so crucial was that LeBron James would be entering the draft.

LeBron James was regarded by many as the greatest player in the history of high school basketball and seen as the chosen one to replace Michael Jordan as the game's greatest player of all time. He was from Akron, Ohio, and Cleveland fans had the privilege of watching him grow up as a basketball prodigy in their own backyard. The hype surrounding James was so big that his senior year games at St. Vincent St. Mary High School were broadcast on national television, with several of them played at Quicken Loans Arena. Because of his talent, most NBA experts considered James better than 75 percent of the current league's talent before he had even played a game in the league. For the Cavaliers, the chance to pick him signaled a rebirth for the franchise and for the city of Cleveland.

The 2003 NBA draft was regarded as one of the strongest in history. The top five picks produced four of the best players currently playing today. Cleveland selected LeBron James with its pick, and two picks later, Denver selected future all-star Carmelo Anthony from Syracuse. With the fourth

LeBron James, the "Chosen One," arrived in 2003. *Photo by Stephanie Najar.*

Anderson Varejao signs a ball for a fan. *Photo by Betty Cantley.*

pick, the Toronto Raptors selected Chris Bosh, who also remains one of the top players in the game. The fifth pick went to the Miami Heat, who struck gold with their selection, Dwayne Wade. The Heat would eventually pair Wade with Shaquille O'Neal and win the NBA championship just three years later. The draft was loaded with talent, but it was clear that Cleveland was receiving its top prize. Little did anyone realize that seven years later, three of the top players would team up to make up a dream team in Miami.

Mary Schmitt Boyer describes the importance of choosing LeBron James with the number-one pick:

> *It saved basketball in Cleveland. If you look at the value of the team and how much it jumped up in just the first two years he was on the team before Dan Gilbert bought it in 2005…it was clear LeBron was a major factor behind the city's resurgence for its love of basketball.*

Paul Silas would be the first coach to take his shot at coaching LeBron James as a professional. Gordon Gund believed Silas was the right man for the job, given his history as an NBA player and coach prior to coming to Cleveland. Silas had played on two NBA championship teams with the Boston Celtics and Seattle Supersonics, winning a combined three titles. He was also a two-time all-star and had made the All-NBA Defensive Team twice. He had the pedigree to bring winning ways back to Cleveland, as well as guide the young superstar James.

LeBron James's first year as a Cavalier began with a trend that would become all too familiar during his early years in Cleveland. He had a weak supporting cast, with Ricky Davis and Darius Miles more eager to shoot the ball than feed it to the growing phenomenon. Carlos Boozer was a bright spot, as was Cleveland veteran center Zydrunas Ilgauskas, both of whom helped James grow. James and Boozer quickly became one of the strongest tandems in the Eastern Conference.

The Cavaliers finished with thirty-five wins, more than twice as many as the year before. It was clear that even with a weak supporting cast, LeBron was a difference maker. He won the NBA Rookie of the Year Award in a landslide. Later that summer, he would join the U.S. Olympic basketball team and gain further valuable playing and team experience. He was taught that it takes more than just hype to win, as the heavily favored U.S. team failed to win the gold medal for the first time in over twelve years of Olympic play.

The off-season had its share of drama as Carlos Boozer left for Utah in an extremely questionable way that ultimately led to the firing of general manager Jim Paxson. The Cavs filled their need for a veteran starting point guard when they traded Kevin Ollie and Kedrick Brown to Philadelphia for Eric Snow. They pulled off another key trade with the Orlando Magic that brought eventual starting power forward and fan favorite Anderson Varejao to town. At the time of the trade, Varejao was simply a throw-in. Little did fans know that he would become a staple of Cavs basketball for the next ten years.

LeBron picked up where he had left off the year before and started his second season red-hot. After losing their first three games by narrow margins, James led the Cavs on a six-game winning streak. At the halfway point of the season, James was putting up incredible numbers, and the Cavaliers sat near the top of the Eastern Conference standings with a 24-15 record. The rest of the league was starting to take notice as James was voted in as a starter for that year's All-Star Game. Things continued to go well, and the Cavs' record had grown to 31-21 by February 23, 2005. Paul Silas seemed to have everything in control, but then the Cavaliers suddenly went on a six-game losing streak. They ended up losing nine games out of twelve and slipped to 34-30 on the season. It was at this time that new owner Dan Gilbert made the shocking move to fire Paul Silas. The Cavs never recovered and ended up finishing the season at 42-40 under interim coach Brendan Malone. They narrowly missed the playoffs, and their next move would have to be landing the right head coach. LeBron showed he could play at an elite level, but he needed the right team around him and the right coach to guide them.

Because of Dan Gilbert's confidence in him, Mike Brown was hired as the new head coach before a GM was even selected. Mike had begun his basketball career as an unpaid video intern with the Denver Nuggets. He would spend five years as their video coordinator before joining the coaching staffs of the Washington Wizards and San Antonio Spurs. Brown was with San Antonio when the Spurs won the NBA championship in 2003. It was different from the life of fame and high expectations that LeBron James had been expecting. For the Cavs fans, it would be interesting to see if the two personalities would mesh. Under Mike Brown, LeBron would grow to be one of the best defensive players in the game. With the proper coach in place, it was then up to Ferry to start bringing the needed supporting talent to go with James on the court.

Former player Danny Ferry took over as the new GM. Ferry wanted to bring the best talent to Cleveland, but after premier players such as Ray Allen and Michael Redd signed elsewhere, he had to settle for B-level free agents Larry Hughes, Donyell Marshall and Damon Jones. Despite not getting

Anderson Varejao in pre-game warm-ups. *Photo by Betty Cantley.*

The San Antonio Spurs looked to stop the red-hot Cavs in 2007. *Courtesy of www.vpeterpress.com.*

Quicken Loans Arena gets ready for Game Four of the 2007 NBA Finals. *Photo by Betty Cantley.*

the top-tier free agents, the Cavaliers were expected to compete fiercely for a playoff spot that season. All three players could score, but they lacked defensive skill, and it was not the ideal scenario for Brown's first season. It would be his task as head coach to find a way to make it work.

The Cavaliers began the 2005–06 season on a tear by winning nine of their first eleven games, highlighted by an eight-game winning streak. The new players were meshing well with one another, and LeBron James continued to get better with each game. James also had the incredible ability to improve the players around him. A month after the first winning streak, the Cavs went on to win another six games and increased their record to an impressive 17-9. After hitting a rough patch midseason, they recovered with a seven-game winning streak and headed into the All-Star Break with a 31-21 record. Some pundits—both national and local—were starting to call the Cavaliers "Team Streak."

James took his place as one of the best players in the game by winning the MVP award in the All-Star Game that year, the youngest player ever to do so. He scored twenty-nine points to go with six assists in the game, leading the East to a double-digit, come-from-behind victory. The league, the nation and the entire sports world were starting to notice that James was beginning his ascension to greatness.

The Cavaliers remained hot under James's incredible playing and went on another nine-game winning streak before the season ended. They finished with fifty wins for the first time in years, and LeBron James was about to enter the NBA Playoffs for the first time with one of the hottest teams in basketball by his side. It was an incredible turnaround for a franchise that had won only seventeen games just three years prior. The moves by Gilbert and Ferry had worked during the regular season—now it was time to see if their roster could take the next step in the upcoming NBA playoffs.

In the first round, the Cavs would have to face the Washington Wizards, who were led by a trio of superstars in Antawn Jamison, Gilbert Arenas and Caron Butler. LeBron James was coming off his best season as a pro, and many wondered how he would handle the pressure of his first playoff series. The twenty-one-year-old James ended all doubt in Game One as he scored thirty-two points to go with eleven assists and eleven rebounds en route to a triple-double. The *wunderkind*'s terrific effort was more than enough to lead the Cavs to a 97–86 victory. LeBron James was quoted after the game as saying, "It's a God-given talent. I don't know how the box score will end up at the end of the game. I just try to go out there and play hard and play my game." The quote showed that James was a team player focused on doing whatever he could to help the team win and not on his own statistics.

The "Big Three" of Washington were too much to handle for Cleveland in the next game, however, as they dropped Game Two 89–84 to even up the series. Game Three took place in Washington, and LeBron James again displayed a masterful performance. The Cavaliers trailed all game but used an incredible fourteen-point fourth-quarter effort from James to get the come-from-behind victory, 97–96. James scored forty-one total points and hit the game-winning shot with 5.7 seconds remaining in the game. It was apparent to the basketball world that James was quickly becoming unstoppable. Head coach Mike Brown summed it up perfectly with his post-game comment: "LeBron James is special." It was short but extremely accurate. The ability of James to hit game-winning shots only increased the comparisons to Michael Jordan.

James followed his stellar Game Three effort with another impressive one in Game Four by scoring thirty-eight points. But it wasn't enough, as he didn't get much help from teammates, and the Wizards won 106–96, once again evening up the series.

Game Five returned the series to Cleveland. The dramatic back-and-forth series was quickly becoming a classic, and this game did not disappoint. The game remained tied after four hard-fought quarters. As overtime began, the fans in attendance at the Q Arena could sense another dramatic conclusion. Gilbert Arenas made two pressure-packed foul shots to put the Wizards ahead with only 3.9 seconds left. Mike Brown called a timeout, and the Cavs drew up their final play. LeBron James received the inbound pass and cut to the hole with enough time to lay in a game-winning shot over Washington defender Michael Ruffin. It was James's second game-winner of the series, and it capped off a forty-five-point performance.

Game Six returned to Washington with the Cavaliers on the brink of advancing to the next round of the playoffs. This game, just like Game Five, went into overtime. Washington had led throughout the majority of the game, but the Cavaliers used a strong second half to force overtime. Anderson Varejao had double-digit rebounds, Larry Hughes chipped in with twelve assists and LeBron had thirty-five points, but the key points came from backup shooting guard Damon Jones. With 4.8 seconds left in overtime and Cleveland down one, Jones's go-ahead jump shot iced the game and put the Cavaliers into the Eastern Conference semifinals against the Detroit Pistons.

Few people outside Cleveland gave the Cavs any chance at defeating the top-seeded Detroit Pistons. Through the first two games, it looked like the skeptics were correct, as the Pistons handled the Cavs easily. With the series returning to Cleveland for Game Three, the Cavaliers were desperate for a victory, and that's just what they got. LeBron James had another triple-double (twenty-one points, ten rebounds and ten assists) to bring Cleveland back into the series. James was proving to be a clutch player when the team needed him the most.

For the second straight game, the Cavaliers were without starting shooting guard Larry Hughes, as he was mourning the loss of his brother. The Cavs played hard for their teammate and used a gritty defensive effort to beat the Pistons 74–72 and even the series. They used Hughes's family situation to become stronger as a team and grow together as men. They were a team united and suddenly a real threat to upset Detroit.

Game Five returned to the Palace at Auburn Hills with the Pistons looking to reclaim the series lead in front of their hometown fans. The Cavs used a thirty-two-point effort by James to upset the Pistons 86–84. James again showed his ability to make those around him better by finding power forward Drew Gooden with twenty-seven seconds left. Gooden was then able to hit the shot that put Cleveland ahead for good. LeBron James was quoted by the

Cleveland Plain Dealer after the game as saying, "They aren't the Big Bad Wolf, and we aren't the Three Little Pigs. We are all grown men, and we know we can beat them!"

Detroit was able to use late offensive rebounds by Rip Hamilton in Game Six to steal the victory and force a Game Seven. The Cavaliers played miserably in Game Seven and were defeated 79–61, ending their magical playoff run. It was a disappointing end, but it showed that, if given another chance, LeBron James could lead the Cavs deeper into the playoffs. He proved he could both set up his teammates and make game-winning shots when called on. It gave the entire team confidence heading into the off-season.

The following season, 2006–07, was a rollercoaster ride that saw the Cavs achieve the same record they had the previous season, 50-32. The biggest difference was that this season, it qualified them for a second seed in the playoffs instead of a fourth seed. This also meant that the Cavs would be on the opposite side of the bracket with Detroit, and the potential rematch would not take place until the Eastern Conference finals. They were on a collision course with Detroit once again.

The good news was that the Cavs were bringing back almost the same roster from the previous season. This continuity allowed them to continue to grow and improve. Mike Brown was doing a fine job of mixing in the veterans with the young talent and strengthening the defense. The season was highlighted by an eight-game winning streak late in the second half. James continued to improve, and by the end of the season he was averaging 27.3 points, 6.7 rebounds and 6 assists per game.

The first-round playoff series was a rematch against Washington. The result was far different from the previous year, however, as Cleveland swept the Wizards with ease in four straight games. Round two would be a tougher task as the Cavs faced Jason Kidd, Vince Carter, Richard Jefferson and the much-improved New Jersey Nets. They won Game One with ease and then used a thirty-six-point performance from James in Game Two to roll past New Jersey and take a 2–0 series lead. New Jersey bounced back at home and won Game Three to climb back in the series.

In Game Four, Larry Hughes chipped in nineteen points alongside LeBron James's thirty points as the Cavs narrowly beat New Jersey 87–85. Two games later, Cleveland finished New Jersey off, advancing to the Eastern Conference finals to once again play the Detroit Pistons. The previous season's loss was still fresh on everyone's mind, but the Cavs were determined to use that as motivation and confidence heading into the rematch. Fred McLeod, a member of the television broadcasting team for the Cavs, shares how he felt about the Cavs' chances of getting past Detroit in the series:

> *It really was a special year in which the brackets set up perfectly for the Cavaliers. I remember vividly when we clinched the division late in the season and Austin Carr crying because he was so happy. It was an emotional moment, and I had to look away because I felt myself becoming emotional as well. Donyell Marshall was red-hot in the series against New Jersey to get the Cavs to the Eastern Conference finals, and it felt as though things were going their way. Mike Brown is such a hardworking coach, and I knew he would have them ready. He works so hard and is such a good man.*

Game One in Detroit ended in dramatic fashion as LeBron James had a chance to put Cleveland ahead in the closing seconds but instead opted to pass off to teammate Donyell Marshall, who promptly missed a three-pointer to give Detroit the win. James would undergo extreme criticism following the game for not taking the shot. Marshall had hit six three-pointers in the game, as well as six against New Jersey a few nights prior, and James saw him wide open for the shot. Despite playing the Pistons tough all night and holding a lead numerous times, the Cavaliers lost the game 79–76. Fred McLeod reveals what it was like having to call that heartbreaking moment:

> *He made the right basketball play. LeBron was correct to pass it to Marshall, who was wide open and standing at his corner sweet spot. LeBron took a lot of heat for that, but it was the right play. Jordan passed it once to win a championship in Phoenix. LeBron James was in a no-win situation there. But again, it's basketball, and those moments and plays are going to happen.*

Game Two would follow almost the exact storyline as the previous night. Once again, the game came down to the end with Cleveland having the ball and a chance to win. This time, LeBron James didn't hesitate to drive the lane and take the game-winning shot. He was fouled hard by numerous Pistons, but the refs chose not to call it, and the Pistons eventually got the rebound, ending Cleveland's chance. The Pistons made their free throws after Mike Brown's technical foul for arguing the no-call on LeBron. Coach Brown was livid, and he had every right to be, as the Pistons were hammering James every time he touched the ball but weren't being penalized. It was one of the worst referring performances in recent memory, and announcer Fred McLeod explains that it was hard to keep his emotions in check:

He was fouled, and it was very hard. Those are times when I defer to my partner, Austin Carr. He can be very emotional but also very factual. He has been there and played, and his word carries serious weight. The officials do a great job most times, but you will have those moments. We try to be fair to them and have even had officials come up to us and thank us for the job we do. They are trying their best, but it is not easy in moments such as those.

The final score matched that of Game One, with Detroit coming out on top 79–76. The Cavaliers used the anger and heartbreak from both of the close losses to come out hungry and aggressive in Game Three back in Cleveland. The series continued to be physical, but the Cavs fought hard and won Games Three and Four to even it up. The series was following an identical timeline of the previous year's, and Game Five was setting up to be every bit as crucial and dramatic.

Game Five took place on May 31, 2007, and thanks to LeBron James, it would go down as one of the greatest basketball playoff games of all time. In one of the greatest playoff efforts in the history of the game, James scored his team's last twenty-five points to lead the Cavs to a 109–107 double-overtime victory. James scored twenty-nine of his team's last thirty, and Detroit had no answer for him. NBA fans everywhere sat in awe as James single-handedly took the game over late in the fourth quarter and carried his teammates to the win. The Pistons had led throughout the night, and if it weren't for the heroic effort of James, they would have easily won. Detroit had stifled James earlier in this series but simply couldn't contain the "Chosen One" on this epic night. James was only twenty-two years old at the time, and Cleveland fans had every reason to believe this was just one of many amazing playoff games they would get to witness from their homegrown hero. Fred McLeod reveals what it was like to watch and be so close to such an amazing game:

I was part of the pre and post-game that night, so I was at the Palace watching it. I had witnessed so many great moments there over the years, but that was truly special. It was a sign that he had arrived and was the real deal. Also, I think it gave us the momentum we needed heading back to Cleveland to put them away in Game Six.

For the second time in two years, the Cavaliers had the chance to put away the Pistons at home in six games. The stakes were even higher for this game because one more win meant a berth in the NBA Finals for the first time in franchise history. Cleveland fans stood at attention all night with their hopes held high that the Cavs would find a way to close it out this year. Cavs owner Dan Gilbert made it known from day one that his sole mission was to reach the NBA Finals, and now because of his young phenomenon, he was only one win away. The Pistons focused all their efforts during the game on trying to stop James. They held him in check through the beginning of the game, but it would only be a matter of time before LeBron broke loose. With the Pistons' attention elsewhere, it allowed rookie sensation Daniel "Boobie" Gibson to get open for several three-pointers. By the night's end, Gibson had hit five three-pointers on his way to a game-high thirty-one points.

Gibson's incredible effort, combined with LeBron James's twenty points, was far too much for Detroit to overcome. For the first time in franchise history, the Cleveland Cavaliers were headed to the NBA Finals. Fans who had attended that night's Indians game at Jacobs Field stood in the walkway between the stadium and arena and watched the celebration on the big screen. After many years of struggling and near misses, the Cavs fans let loose and celebrated as their team could finally be called champions. Even the broadcast team got to share in the excitement. Fred McLeod describes the emotion of the series-clinching win:

> *It was an amazing and emotional night. Boobie Gibson was on fire, and that's when the term "Shoot, Boobie, Shoot!" began. You had seen a team that had worked so hard and deserved the win. It was awesome to look into the gateway plaza and see the fans going crazy with excitement. Cleveland is such a great sports town with loyal, hardworking fans that deserved a winner, and they finally had a team going to the NBA Finals. We have the best fans in sports, and they proved how passionate they were that night.*

Mary Schmitt Boyer explains why the Cavs were finally able to get over the hump and beat Detroit:

> *LeBron was not to be denied as he was on the ascent. He loaded that team on his back and was not going to be denied. The Eastern Conference was weaker that year, and they were able to take advantage of it. The team totally bought into Mike's defensive philosophy. He did such a good job coaching younger players. The stars aligned for the team, and they bought into the entire team philosophy. They were led by a guy on his way up, and they took care of things with a right time-right place mentality.*

This was the first run to the NBA Finals for Cavs fans, and they remember it vividly. CBS radio personality and 92.3 The Fan host Vic Travagliante remembers fondly some of the traditions he had during the epic playoff run:

> *During the run to the playoffs, I would always go to Whitey's, which is located next to where the old Coliseum once was. It was the hotspot for many fans going to the Coliseum for any sporting event or concert before the move to Quicken Loans Arena downtown. I watched every game during that run from Whitey's. I always sat in the corner of the bar and ordered wings with hot sauce and had an adult beverage as I watched every game. I was enthralled by the action on the court and the drama of the games. That was the second time I chased that winning feeling with a team.*

Host of the *Sports Fix* radio show and avid Cleveland sports fan Jerry Mires also recalls his memories of the Cavs' run to the finals:

> *Looking back at it now, we know they were flawed, but at the time we didn't realize it. That was right around the time LeBron started to change. Until that point, there weren't a lot of stories of people catering to him. I'm not trying to take anything away from the Cavs, but I honestly thought the NBA wanted the Cavs to win. Things like referee Tim Donaghy admitting to fixing games—it makes you begin to wonder. The NBA manipulates things the way they want it to keep their star players in the limelight. I really did think the Cavs team would win it all until they got to the finals and the Spurs swept the floors with us. They were guarding LeBron with numerous players, and no one else could step up to help him. The way they beat Detroit made me think that they could win, but I was wrong. I remember laying carpet for a couple relatives of mine and talking with them every day about the series, trying to rationalize ways that the Cavs could come back and win. With LeBron being the chosen one, it seemed like anything was possible. I remember the emotions of getting swept as the games went on. It was the middle of the San Antonio Spurs' run, and there was no stopping them.*

Despite the outcome in the NBA Finals, a sweep by the San Antonio Spurs, the Cavs' run in the 2007 playoffs will always be remembered as the coming-out party for LeBron James. Vic Travagliante recalls his heartbreak when Cleveland fell to the Spurs in the finals:

I attended Game Three of the NBA championship series against the Spurs with my uncle. I had never experienced an event of that magnitude until that evening. It had the pageantry and lights that was promised. I remember that big NBA championship blow-up gimmick that was set in front of the arena. I remember thinking, "Wow, we are here!" My uncle and I had the blessing of sitting eight rows from the scorer's table. I remember Andy V, in the closing seconds of a close game, instead of giving the ball to LeBron, taking two dribbles and trying to spin down the middle of the paint and losing the basketball. I don't think I have ever sworn so much in one sentence—I was very mad. It was a little closer to home for me because growing up, I lived near Akron and played against LeBron in high school a number of times. His entourage and a number of people I would hang out with did cross paths because we had the same friends and still do to this day. I had a little bit of a different interest in it because someone I knew and hung out with on occasion in high school was trying to and possibly could bring Cleveland its first championship in my lifetime and most people's lifetimes. I remember them losing and thinking to myself that it was okay because they would be back next year. I will never make that mistake again.

Austin Carr also gives his take on why the Cavs couldn't get over the hump and bring home the ring:

It was maturity. If LeBron was the player then that he is now, I think we would have gotten over the hump. We just didn't have enough sense of rotations and covering for each other on the floor. We just weren't ready then. We got there because of LeBron, but he couldn't do it by himself. As a team, we couldn't overcome adversity. Nobody expected us to get to the finals, and the San Antonio Spurs were a well-oiled machine. That is just the way it is. We got there, and we just weren't mentally ready for the challenge.

In a matter of four years, the Cavaliers had managed to rebound from having the league's worst record to reaching the NBA Finals. It was a remarkable turnaround, and now the only question was not whether they could get back to the finals but if they could win it all when they did. One thing was for sure: we were all ready to bear witness to what was to come.

Chapter 10

The Trade

The Cavaliers didn't have too long to celebrate their run to the NBA Finals before they had to start dealing with serious roster issues. Two key members of the team were planning to hold out for contract extensions. Both Anderson Varejao and Sasha Pavlovic had contracts set to expire soon and wanted to renew for more money. The Cavaliers didn't seem eager at first, and it looked like it might be a long off-season.

With the exception of the holdout drama, it was a quiet off-season. The Cavs signed only one free agent of note, bringing in Devin Brown, a five-year veteran who had spent time with San Antonio, Denver, Utah and New Orleans. Brown was a solid backup shooting guard, which, given the Larry Hughes injury concerns, was very important.

The night before the opening game, the team received some good news: the organization had come to terms with Sasha Pavlovic on a contract extension. Although he wouldn't be ready for the first few games, he would return to action in time for the six-game West Coast road trip. The Cavs lost their opening game to the Dallas Mavericks but bounced back a few nights later at home against the New York Knicks. They split the six-game road trip with wins against the Golden State Warriors, Sacramento Kings and Los Angeles Clippers and losses against the Phoenix Suns, Utah Jazz and Denver Nuggets.

They received some good news when they returned home from their trip, as sources noted that Anderson Varejao was getting closer to ending his holdout. It was hoped that he would be coming back soon because they

Boobie Gibson speaks with Kenny Roda and Michael Reghi. *Photo by Kenny Roda.*

Delonte West was a huge pickup in 2008. *Photo by Betty Cantley.*

were sorely missing his energy off the bench. The team ran into a stumbling block, however, when team leader LeBron James went down with an injury during the November 28, 2007 game against the Pistons in Detroit. It was a costly blow, but the doctor said he would be out only a couple weeks. During that stretch, the Cavaliers lost six straight games. It was a bad omen that would become more apparent four seasons later.

James was set to return on December 11, 2007, which also happened to be the same night Anderson Varejao would end his holdout and rejoin the team. Getting their two best players back on the same night had Cleveland fans excited, and they packed Quicken Loans Arena to witness the contest against the Indiana Pacers that night. For the first time in his career, LeBron James decided not to start the game. He thought it would be best if he came off the bench with Anderson, thus shielding him from receiving the boos from the crowd that often accompany a long holdout. It was another sign that LeBron was becoming a great teammate and maturing into a superstar both on and off the court. The Cavaliers managed to win the game 118–105.

Despite the return of James and Varejao, the Cavs were still struggling to find their stride and slumped into a 14-17 record as the calendar turned to 2008. It was at this point that they finally snapped out of their slump and got hot. It began with a four-game winning streak in which they defeated the Atlanta Hawks, Sacramento Kings, Toronto Raptors and Seattle Supersonics. They then lost a close game in Atlanta against the Hawks before going on a five-game winning streak, including an overtime win against the Memphis Grizzlies and a double-overtime win against the Charlotte Bobcats. At the end of these two winning streaks, their record had improved drastically to 23-19.

They then started winning as many as they lost and entered the last week of February with a 30-24 record. There had been rumors for some time that the Cavaliers' chemistry wasn't as good as it had been in previous years. Despite the winning record, general manager Danny Ferry still felt that the team needed a shake-up in order to return to the later rounds of the playoffs.

On February 21, 2008, Danny Ferry pulled off a blockbuster deal that no one saw coming. It was three-team trade with the Chicago Bulls and Seattle Supersonics that would change 25 percent of the Cavaliers' roster. The Cavs traded Donyell Marshall and Ira Newble to the Seattle Supersonics, while also sending Shannon Brown, Drew Gooden, Larry Hughes and Cedric Simmons to the Chicago Bulls. The Bulls traded Joe Smith, Ben Wallace and a 2009 second-round draft pick (Danny Green was later selected) to the

Anderson Varejao poses for the media. *Photo by Kenny Roda.*

Boobie Gibson addresses the media. *Photo by Kenny Roda.*

Christian Eyenga. *Photo by Kenny Roda.*

Cleveland Cavaliers and also sent Adrian Griffin to the Seattle Supersonics, who traded Wally Szczerbiak and Delonte West to the Cavs. It was a crucial trade that brought high risk but also the chance for very high reward.

Ben Wallace, a key piece in the previous post-season runs for the Detroit Pistons, hadn't been with the Bulls long, and it was surprising that they were so quick to deal him away. A powerful center and power forward, his presence down low with Zydrunas Ilgauskas would become a major plus for the Cavaliers. The addition of Delonte West was not to be overlooked either. West might have had his quirks, but the kid could play! He was quick with the ball and didn't turn it over. He could shoot and pass with the best of them and also played incredible defense. West was a huge pickup that would solidify the backcourt. Joe Smith, the first overall pick in the 1995 NBA draft, was determined that he still had something left in the tank and could provide several rebounds off the bench each and every night.

Perhaps the player the fans were most excited to welcome into the fold was Wally Szczerbiak. His dad, Walt, was a former ABA player, and basketball was in the Szczerbiak blood. Wally attended college at Miami University in nearby Oxford, Ohio. In his junior season, 1997–98, he burst onto the scene as one of college basketball's leading scorers, averaging 24.4 points per game and earning first-team All-MAC honors despite missing several games with a broken wrist.

In his senior season, 1998–99, he averaged 24.2 points per game and led the Redhawks to the NCAA tournament as the tenth overall seed. Szczerbiak scored a career-high 43 points in a first-round win over seventh-seeded University of Washington. He followed that up with 24 points in the second round against highly rated second seed Utah, leading the Redhawks to the Sweet 16, where they would eventually lose to Kentucky. In addition to being named MAC Player of the Year, he was also named first-team All-American by *Basketball News* and *Sports Illustrated,* as well as second-team All-American by the Associated Press. He finished his career at Miami University as the school's second all-time leading scorer with 1,847 points. So beloved was Szczerbiak that in 2001, the school retired his jersey, and in 2009, he was inducted into the Miami University Hall of Fame. Also, in 2013, he was inducted into the Ohio Basketball Hall of Fame.

The Minnesota Timberwolves selected Szczerbiak sixth overall in the 1999 NBA draft. He was a key piece on a team that featured Kevin Garnett and would eventually reach the Western Conference finals. His best year as a pro was in 2002, when he was a coaches' selection to the Western Conference All-Star team. His shooting was so good and prolific at times that he tied a Timberwolves franchise record of forty-four points on April 13, 2003. Despite a good career with the Timberwolves, economics and politics took him away from Minnesota, and he spent short stints in both Boston and Seattle before coming to Cleveland.

It was a gutsy move by Ferry, but it was one he had to make to strengthen the team for another run deep into the playoffs. Hughes had been too injury-prone and inconsistent, making him expendable. He wasn't the solid number-two scoring threat that the Cavs needed him to be when they signed him to a large free-agent deal in the summer of 2005. And Drew Gooden, picked fourth overall in the draft several years earlier, had never quite reached his potential. He was loved by fans and teammates, but Ferry knew that the trade wouldn't be possible unless Gooden was included.

Mary Schmitt Boyer gives her reaction to the blockbuster trade:

> *It was quite a shock, but it brought in some toughness. Wallace was a tough presence to have around in a positive way. He was scary and intimidating but at the same time made for a great interview because he was always willing to talk. Delonte West may have run into some problems later on, but*

when he was on the court, he really helped the team and played well. Danny Ferry didn't believe that the current roster before the trade was going to be good enough to reach the finals, and he knew this move was needed. I think he wanted to mix up the chemistry, and he was not afraid to do so. It was new blood and new toughness, and the fans were excited.

The Cavs reacted well to the new cast of players as they won their first seven of nine after the trade. It was going to take time to mesh, but the new players showed they were ready to play and contribute. They finished the regular season at 45-37 and looked poised for another run at the Eastern Conference championship.

The Cavs' first-round opponent was a familiar foe in the Washington Wizards. It would be the third straight season in which they faced Washington in the opening round. The Wizards had their big three ready, with Gilbert Arenas, Caron Butler and Antawn Jamison poised to do everything they could to avenge last year's loss. The Cavs were ready for the Wizards to come out strong and fight them hard the entire game. It took a thirty-two-point performance by LeBron James, but in the end, the Cavaliers took Game One by the score of 93–86. The Wizards had led after the first and third quarters, but the Cavs used a twenty-eight-point fourth quarter to overcome them for good. Delonte West helped out with sixteen points, five rebounds, five assists and two steals in his first playoff game as a Cavalier.

Game Two was not nearly as close, as the Cavaliers blew out the Wizards 116–86. It was a thirty-point victory that proved how good Cleveland could be when running on all cylinders. LeBron James had another incredible night, racking up thirty points, twelve assists, two blocked shots and nine rebounds. Wally Szczerbiak, who was starting at shooting guard while Delonte West ran the point, also chipped in with two three-pointers on his way to a fifteen-point night. The Cavs would travel to Washington with a commanding 2–0 lead in the best-of-seven series.

Washington returned the favor in Game Three and blew out the Cavaliers at home by a score of 108–72. LeBron James had twenty-two points, but only one other Cavs player was able to score in the double digits. It was a poor effort that allowed Washington back in the series.

Game Four was a back-and-forth affair that would come down to the wire once again. The Wizards held a four-point lead after the first quarter, but the Cavs then outscored them 30–16 in the second quarter to take a ten-point lead into halftime. Washington cut into the lead in the third quarter and trailed by just seven heading into the fourth. They continued to make it close, but in the end, the Cavaliers managed to hang on for a 100–97 win. It gave them a stranglehold on the series, which was heading back home for Game Five.

It was another impressive effort by LeBron James as he had thirty-four points to go along with twelve rebounds, seven assists and two steals. Delonte West once again showed that he could be a great number-two scoring threat behind LeBron as he chipped in with twenty-one points, five assists and three steals. Game Five back in Cleveland saw Washington slip by with a razor-thin win by a score of 88–87. James scored with ease again, finishing with thirty-four points and ten rebounds. It was an amazing effort from James, but it just wasn't enough, and the series was headed back to Washington for Game Six.

The Wizards used a thirty-one-point first quarter to take an early four-point lead in Game Six. The Cavs held the Washington offense in check in the second quarter, allowing only seventeen points, and took a 56–48 lead into halftime. They were only twenty-four minutes away from reaching the next round, and they came out of halftime fully intent on shutting Washington down for good. They outscored the Wizards 23–16 in the third quarter and took a fifteen-point lead heading into the final frame. Washington managed to cut into the lead a tiny bit, but the Cavaliers were just too much to overcome and won the game 105–88. They were headed back to the Eastern Conference semifinals for the third straight year.

The series-clinching Game Six win was highlighted by a twenty-seven-point scoring effort from LeBron and a twenty-six-point effort from Wally Szczerbiak, who hit an incredible six three-pointers and broke the spirit of the Wizards and their fans. Boobie Gibson also scored twenty-two points off the bench, including four three-pointers of his own. The Cavaliers would need the momentum and positive energy, as they were about to face the team with the NBA's best record.

With the major off-season acquisitions of perennial all-stars Kevin Garnett and Ray Allen, the Boston Celtics had finished with a record of 66-16 and posted the best single-season turnaround in NBA history, improving by forty-two wins over the previous season's total. Kevin Garnett was named NBA Defensive Player of the Year, while Danny Ainge, who executed "the most dramatic NBA turnaround ever," was named Executive of the Year. When joined with Paul Pierce, the trio quickly became known as the "Big Three." This was the first team to form a super group of talent via free-agent acquisitions and trades. They also had a highly talented rookie point guard from Kentucky, Rajon Rondo.

The Cavaliers were going to have their work cut out for them, as Boston was the heavy favorite to win the NBA championship. The Celtics were coming off a surprisingly grueling series against the Atlanta Hawks in which the Hawks shocked everyone by forcing a final Game Seven. Not surprisingly, Boston showed signs of fatigue in Game One, and the Cavaliers hung in there until the very end. A clutch shot by Kevin Garnett in the closing minute was enough to seal the win for Boston, 76–72.

Cleveland couldn't recover in time from the close Game One loss and got blown out in Game Two, 89–73. The physical play by Boston was too much for Cleveland to overcome, as LeBron James went just eight for forty-two from the field in those first two games. The series was on its way back to Cleveland, and the Cavaliers would have to find an answer quickly.

Cleveland entered Game Three in desperate need of a victory. A three-game deficit would be too much for any team to come back from, especially against the league's best team. The Cavs weren't taking any chances. They jumped out to an early 32–13 lead in the first quarter and never looked back. They steamrolled the Celtics all night en route to a 108–84 victory. LeBron James and Delonte West had twenty-one points each in the win. LeBron stayed hot in Game Four with another twenty-one points, and the Cavaliers pulled off the victory 88–77 to even up the series at two games apiece.

The pivotal Game Five of this epic series returned to the TD Garden in Boston. Cleveland was suddenly full of confidence, and the series was up for grabs. The Cavs used a high-energy defensive effort to take a 46–43 halftime lead. They were shutting down the Big Three and looked to have an excellent chance to steal one on the road. However, a familiar problem then crept up on them as they once again failed to come out ready for the second half. They couldn't keep pace with the Celtics after Boston coach Doc Rivers made some key adjustments. Boston outscored the Cavaliers 29–17 in the third quarter and took a nine-point lead into the final quarter.

LeBron and the Cavs fought hard to make it close, but in the end, they dropped Game Five, 97–89. It was a frustrating loss for the Cavs as they had fought hard all night, but the weak third-quarter effort was their downfall. LeBron scored thirty-five points and West twenty-one in the losing effort. They received almost no help at all from the bench. The lack of adjustments to start the second half did not speak well for Mike Brown, as it was clear he was getting out-coached by Doc Rivers.

The Cavs' defense stepped up big in Game Six back in Cleveland by holding the Celtics to only sixty-nine points. Cleveland swarmed Boston shooters all night long and forced a deciding Game Seven by taking Game

Six, 74–69. LeBron took matters into his own hands by putting up thirty-two points, twelve rebounds and six assists. The series was headed back to Boston for a decisive Game Seven.

Few words in sports excite fans more than "Game Seven." This had been a classic series already, and the Game Seven showdown was set to capture the attention of the nation. Boston had the best record in the league and was the heavy favorite to win it all. Cleveland was the defending champ with arguably the world's best player. It was a battle of two heavyweights; they had already gone six brutal rounds, and the fans were set for a thrilling finish.

Game Seven looked like it might be a blowout as Boston came out of the gate with all guns blazing. By halftime, the Celtics led 50–40 and had Cleveland beat in almost every category. But it was Mike Brown making the crucial adjustments at the half this time, and the Cavs came roaring back in the third quarter to cut the lead to five points heading into the fourth and final quarter. An incredible duel was developing between Paul Pierce and LeBron James. Pierce finished with forty-one points, while James scored forty-five. In the end, Boston did just enough to win the game 97–92 and take the series. It sent the Cavs home and ended their bid to repeat as Eastern Conference champions.

It was a hard-fought series for Cleveland in which the Cavs surprised many with how well they played and how far they pushed Boston. It was encouraging to see the new players mesh so well together, and many thought they could only get better with a full off-season of working out and fine-tuning. LeBron only had two years left on his contract, and one final push for a championship was set to begin in MVP fashion!

Chapter 11

The MVP

The Cavs were on a mission to make up for their early exit in the 2008 playoffs with a dominant 2008–09 season. They had the makings of a great team as the players they traded for midseason were starting to gel nicely with the established players toward the end of the playoff run. Many people felt that if they had had more time to play together, they could have even upset the Celtics. The task for Danny Ferry was clear: he needed to find one more piece and then put it all together for another serious run at the title.

The off-season started off with the Cavs taking J.J. Hickson out of North Carolina State University with their first pick in the draft. Hickson was the nineteenth pick overall and came with mild expectations. He could play both power forward and center and was expected to soak up minutes when called on from the bench. He had potential, and he would be given the time to develop and improve behind the veterans.

The big move came on August 13, 2008, when the Cavaliers took part in a three-team trade with the Oklahoma City Thunder and Milwaukee Bucks that saw the departure of Damon Jones and Joe Smith and the arrival of sharpshooting point guard Mo Williams from the Bucks. Williams was a quality point guard who knew how to generate points with a variety of passes and smart shots. He was quick off the dribble and could create his own shot when needed. He was the perfect complement to Delonte West in the backcourt.

LeBron James suddenly had numerous weapons in a loaded starting lineup. In the backcourt, the Cavs had Mo Williams running the point with

LeBron James warms up. *Photo by Michell Durosko.*

LeBron James is concerned at the lack of help he is receiving. *Photo by Michell Durosko.*

LeBron James meets with fans before the game. *Photo by Michell Durosko.*

Delonte West playing shooting guard, while twin towers Ben Wallace and Zydrunas Ilgauskas were down low crashing the boards nightly. They were also stacked on the bench with Anderson Varejao, Sasha Pavlovic, Boobie Gibson and Wally Szczerbiak. Cleveland was picked by many to contend with Boston for the best record in the Eastern Conference.

The Cavs would be tested right away, as opening night was back in Boston at the TD Garden, where they would face the defending NBA champions. The Celtics picked up where they left off, and despite a great effort by Cleveland, they managed to get the 90–85 victory. It was clear that the Celtics would remain the team to beat, but only for a little longer.

The Cavaliers split their next two games with a win at home against Charlotte and a loss on the road in New Orleans against the Hornets. It was after the loss to the Hornets that the Cavs caught fire, and they remained red-hot all season long. They rolled off an eight-game winning streak highlighted by wins over the Dallas Mavericks, Chicago Bulls, Indiana Pacers, Denver Nuggets and Utah Jazz. They had a quick stumbling block with a loss to the Pistons in Detroit but then quickly bounced back with an eleven-game winning streak that pushed their record to 20-3. They then lost

LeBron James nails another three-pointer. *Photo by Michell Durosko.*

LeBron James getting ready to ball-fake and then drive to the hole. *Photo by Michell Durosko.*

LeBron James blowing a kiss to his mom. *Photo by Michell Durosko.*

on the road to the Atlanta Hawks before winning six more in a row. They were dominating their opponents, and by the time the calendar turned to 2009, they held a 26-5 record. They also held a perfect home record that stood until the Lakers beat them on February 8. Even with the loss, the Cavs held an impressive 39-10 record and were well on their way to locking up the first overall seed in the playoffs.

They remained red-hot down the stretch with numerous winning streaks, including an impressive thirteen-game winning streak that lasted into late March. Perhaps most impressive was an April 12, 2009 win against Boston in which they pounded the Celtics 107–76. The thirty-one-point win was a clear statement that the Cavaliers had emerged as the absolute best team in the NBA. They finished the regular season with a franchise-best record of 66-16. It was also the best record of any team in the NBA that year. It locked up home field advantage throughout the playoffs and gave Cleveland an enormous amount of momentum heading into the first round.

LeBron James's season was so good that it earned him his first league MVP award. He averaged 28.4 points, 7.6 rebounds and 7.2 assists per game. He was the best player on the court every night and the main reason the Cavaliers enjoyed so much success. It was nice to see the national media finally put aside their negative bias against Cleveland and grant LeBron the well-deserved award.

The supporting cast for LeBron also stepped up huge and played a major role in the incredible regular-season run. Mo Williams averaged 17.8 points a night and finally provided that much-needed number-two scoring threat behind James. A healthy Zydrunas Ilgauskas also continued to improve, chipping in with 12.9 points and 7.5 rebounds a night. Delonte West continued to bring his high-energy defense and killer instinct to the court every night, averaging 11.7 points a night to go with 3.5 assists and 1.5 steals. The Cavs were a serious threat to win the title as they headed into the 2009 playoffs.

They opened up the playoffs against longtime playoff rival the Detroit Pistons. Things were vastly different from just two short years earlier. The Pistons had aged and were no longer the powerhouse they once were. Detroit was the eighth seed and seen as a heavy underdog against the highly favored Cavaliers.

The Cavs jumped out to a quick lead in the series by winning the first two games at home, pounding the Pistons 102–84 and 94–82. The series then headed to the Palace at Auburn Hills, where the Pistons hoped to make a comeback. Cleveland continued to roll, however, polishing off Detroit with wins of 79–68 and 99–78. The first three games were such blowouts that by the time Game Four rolled around, Pistons fans didn't even bother to show up, and more than half the crowd in Detroit consisted of Cavs fans. It was such a magical season that Cleveland fans had no problems driving two and half hours to the Palace to support their team!

LeBron James continued to look amazing in the playoffs, scoring an average of thirty-two points a game in the series against Detroit. The Cavs were red-hot and ready to take on their second-round opponent, the Atlanta Hawks.

With stars such as Joe Johnson, Josh Smith and Mike Bibby, the Atlanta Hawks were seen as a very formidable opponent coming into the second-round series. Many broadcasters considered them good enough to push the Cavaliers to at least six, if not seven, games. But the Cavs weren't affected by the hype, and they went right out and swept the Hawks in four games with relative ease. Atlanta just couldn't compete with the high-powered Cleveland attack. The Cavs had won eight straight playoff games and were looking simply unstoppable.

Heading into the conference semifinals, everyone around the league expected a Cleveland versus Boston rematch. But the Orlando Magic had a different idea and upset the Celtics in seven games. The Magic were young and talented, but few thought they had what it took to hang with the Cavaliers. Little did anyone know that we were headed for a classic series.

Game One was in Cleveland, and the Cavs jumped out to a huge 63–48 lead at halftime. Everything looked in control until Orlando came out in the third quarter and seemingly couldn't miss a shot. The Magic were suddenly red-hot, outscoring the Cavaliers 30–19 in the third quarter. They remained hot in the fourth and had a 107–106 lead with only a few seconds to go. A last-second desperation shot by Mo Williams rattled in and out, and just like that, the Cavs had lost their first playoff game and were suddenly down in the series. Cleveland had wasted a forty-nine-point masterpiece by LeBron James, as the bench provided only five points. It was a shocking and heartbreaking loss.

Game Two followed almost the exact same script as Game One. The Cavaliers once again jumped out to a big lead and led 30–16 after the first quarter. Sadly, just like in Game One, the Magic came roaring back and held a 95–93 lead with only one second to go. Hedo Turkoglu had just hit a clutch shot to give the Magic the lead and take the wind out of the Cleveland crowd. Coach Mike Brown drew up one last play to try and either tie the game or go for the win in the regulation. What followed will forever be one of the great moments in Cleveland sports history. Mo Williams inbounded the ball to LeBron James, who stood twenty-five feet from the basket. James caught the ball, turned and put up a shot that would go down easy and send the Cleveland fans into a frenzy of excitement! It was, at the time, the most defining moment in the young man's career. It also summed up why he had been voted league MVP.

The Cavs dropped Game Three in Orlando by a score of 99–89. The refereeing was horrible all night, and the Cavaliers could not stay out of foul trouble because of it. The Magic suddenly had a stranglehold on the series. They continued to get clutch shots and not allow anyone but LeBron James to score on them. Mo Williams was having a very disappointing series and wasn't providing the needed help for the Cavaliers to compete. If Williams didn't improve in a hurry, and the Cleveland bench didn't wake up out of its slumber, the Cavaliers were in serious trouble.

Game Four in Orlando was another classic that came right down to the wire. Dwight Howard continued to dominate down low, causing the Cavs to force a double team on him and allow Orlando to hit open three-pointers. It was a double-edged sword, and Cleveland was getting sliced by it every time. Rafer Alston was able to cash in on the open looks caused by the Howard double team, scoring twenty-six points to go along with Howard's twenty-seven.

LeBron James always plays with much swagger and emotion. *Photo by Michell Durosko.*

Cleveland hung tough all night, and with less than a minute to go, it was still anyone's game. The Cavs led 98–97 with only six seconds left in the game. LeBron James had just hit two clutch foul shots to give them the lead—now they just needed one defensive stop and the series would be tied at two. After the twenty-second timeout, most everyone thought that since they were down only one, the Magic would be sure to get it down low to Howard and let him try to drive for the win. Instead, it was Hedo Turkoglu driving the lane before kicking out to a well-covered Rashard Lewis, who managed to hit a three-pointer with a hand in his face to give Orlando the 100–98 lead with only 4.1 seconds to go. It was that kind of series for Orlando; everything they did seemed to go right. It was crushing for the Cavaliers, as they had played so well all night.

But with 4.1 seconds left, the game was far from over, and the Cavaliers had one last chance to try for the tie or go for the win. They got the ball into LeBron, who drove the lane and got fouled while putting up the shot. He missed it, but he would have a chance to make two foul shots with only half a second remaining to send the game into overtime. LeBron, with ice in his veins, calmly nailed both foul shots to send the game into overtime. It was a pressure-packed moment handled brilliantly by the game's best player.

Orlando jumped out to a quick lead in overtime, as two dunks by Howard and a Mickael Pietrus three-pointer had the Cavaliers in deep whole. James kept the Cavs in the game by making his foul shots and another clutch three-pointer. The Magic again used their dominant big man Howard down low and built a four-point lead with only six seconds to go. LeBron James nailed a three-pointer to cut the lead down to one with three seconds to go, but after a couple Rashard Lewis fouls shots, the Magic came out with the 116–114 win and took a commanding 3–1 lead in the series.

James again played amazing in the loss, scoring forty-four points to go along with twelve rebounds and seven assists. Zydrunas Ilgauskas continued to have all kinds of problems with stopping Howard, and his weak play was absolutely killing the Cavaliers' chances of winning. James had been playing the best basketball of his career, and the Cavaliers were still down 3–1 in the series. Things were not looking good as they returned home for Game Five. The Cavaliers were wasting one of the best playoff series performances of all time from James.

Game Five proved to be every bit as wild and intense as the first four. The Cavaliers again jumped out to a huge lead in the first quarter. After one frame of play, they led 35–18. Just like the previous games, the Cavaliers once again blew the lead and let Orlando outscore them 37–21 in the second quarter. The teams played each other close to even in the third, which set up another dramatic fourth-quarter finish. Down the street at the Wolfstein Center, comedian Jeff Dunham was keeping the hometown crowd updated with scores between each joke.

The game was nip and tuck throughout the fourth quarter until the Cavaliers finally pulled away in the end with a 112–102 victory. James was again magnificent as he poured in thirty-seven points to go with fourteen rebounds and twelve assists. It was another playoff triple-double for the reigning MVP. Mo Williams was able to contribute as well, chipping in with twenty-four points of his own. The bench was again a cause for concern, however, as it contributed only fifteen points. The Cavaliers had managed to stave off elimination for one more game but would need a road win in Orlando to stay alive.

Game Six in Orlando turned out to be a nightmare for the Cavaliers as the Magic jumped out to a big lead and never looked back. The one constant in the series was Dwight Howard flexing his muscle and having big games every night. The problem for the Cavs was that each game, it was a different player stepping up big to help Howard carry the load. If they focused on Lewis, then Alston or someone else would beat them. The Cavaliers simply couldn't catch a break, and that was evident as they were trailing 58–40 at halftime. Their spirit was broken, and they were running out of answers.

They never got much closer in the second half, and Orlando won Game Six by a score of 103–90, clinching the series. It was a heartbreaking end to what had been a great season. The Cavs had the best record in the league and possessed the league's best player. It came as a shock to numerous pundits around the league as well. Nike was running a puppet commercial that all but directly indicated that the NBA Finals would be the Los Angeles Lakers and Kobe Bryant versus the Cleveland Cavaliers and LeBron James. No one expected the Magic with their big man Howard and group of red-hot shooters to knock off the highly touted Cavaliers.

What made things even more painful for the Cavs was that LeBron James had a truly epic series. He played out of his mind all six games and almost single-handedly beat the Orlando Magic. He averaged an unheard-of 38.5 points a game to go along with 8.3 rebounds and eight assists. It was a shame that such an incredible effort would be wasted on a loss. LeBron ripped his jersey off of his body as he walked to the locker room after the Game Six loss. It was the first sign of frustration from the chosen one.

The Magic went on to lose in only five games to the Los Angeles Lakers and Kobe Bryant. It was a lackluster series that had fans and media members left wondering what they could have seen with a classic Kobe versus LeBron matchup instead.

Mary Schmitt Boyer gives her take on why the Cavs came up short: "Everyone got hot at the right time for Orlando. It was a bad matchup as the double teams on Howard led to countless open threes by guys like Rashard Lewis, who was playing out of his mind in that series." Austin Carr adds, "It was a bad matchup—that's just all it was—and we couldn't overcome it. That was heartbreaking."

The Cavs would enter desperation mode as the off-season began. The upcoming season was the last on LeBron James's contract, and the talk was fast and furious that he would be leaving town at the end of the season. If that was the case, the Cavaliers had only one more chance to win the NBA title with James. No one knew what James would do, but it wasn't worth hoping, so Danny Ferry went out and traded for longtime veteran Shaquille O'Neal. "Shaq" was a four-time NBA champion with the Lakers and Heat, and many saw him as the final piece the Cavaliers needed to achieve their championship dreams. In order to obtain O'Neal from the Phoenix Suns, they had to trade Ben Wallace and Sasha Pavlovic. Sasha had pretty much disappeared from the lineup the season before, and the chance to grab O'Neal was too large to pass up.

To go along with O'Neal, Ferry also signed free-agent guards Anthony Parker and Jamario Moon. The Cavs were loading up once again for one final push at the title while LeBron was still on the roster. The pressure was intense to get it done now before it was too late. They were coming off of a season in which they held the best record, so they knew they were capable of getting into the playoffs again. But they would also have to deal with Delonte West's legal problems off the court.

The Cavs' bid to repeat as the league's best team got off to a horrible start with losses at home against the Boston Celtics and on the road against the Toronto Raptors. However, they rebounded from the rough start to win three in a row and then eight of their next ten. They stayed hot with two more winning streaks of seven and thirteen games. By the All-Star Break, they held a league-best record of 43-11. They were clicking on all cylinders again and looked to be a serious contender to return to the NBA Finals if things remained the same.

Things would not remain the same, however, as Danny Ferry felt the Cavaliers needed one more key piece added to the starting lineup in time for the final playoff push. On February 17, 2010, the Cavs made one more trade. As part of a three-team deal, the Cavs sent Zydrunas Ilgauskas, Emir Preldzic and a 2010 first-round draft pick (Lazar Hayward was later selected) to the Washington Wizards; the Los Angeles Clippers traded Sebastian Telfair to the Cavs and Al Thornton to the Wizards; and the Wizards traded Antawn Jamison to the Cavs and Drew Gooden to the Clippers. For the Cavs, the trade simply meant Zydrunas Ilgauskas for Antawn Jamison. The trade of "Z" was not as shocking as it seemed because it was well known that the Wizards would instantly cut him due to salary cap issues, and within thirty days he would be a free agent with full intent to once again sign with the Cavaliers, which is exactly what happened on March 23, 2010. Essentially, the Cavs received Antawn Jamison for nothing.

The Cavaliers stayed hot after the trade for Jamison and the reacquisition of Ilgauskas and finished with a record of 61-21, the best overall record in the Eastern Conference once again. They were on a separate side of the bracket from Orlando, so many believed there would be a rematch of the previous year's classic series. The problem was that the Boston Celtics were on the same side of the bracket as Cleveland, so a possible showdown with the Cavs' arch nemesis was forecasted for the second round.

LeBron James was once again named the league's MVP. He had another stellar season as he averaged 29.7 points a game along with 8.6 assists and 7.3 rebounds. If this was indeed going to be his last season, James was going out with a bang! He was now a back-to-back MVP award winner, as well as an All-Star Game MVP. He was saving the last open spot on his résumé for NBA Finals MVP, and he was determined that his final season as a Cavalier would fill that void.

It seemed as though everything was going according to plan as the Cavs took care of eighth-seeded Chicago. The Bulls were actually a lot better than their record indicated, and they would continue to improve with future league MVP Derrick Rose leading the way. However, this season and series belonged to the Cavaliers, who disposed of the Bulls in five games. Of special interest in the series was the fact that LeBron James hurt his elbow, an injury that would rear its ugly head in the next series against the Boston Celtics.

The Celtics still had their "Big Three" and posed a formidable threat for the Cavaliers in the second round. Memories of the epic seven-game series from just two years earlier were still fresh in everyone's minds. Cleveland fans hoped and prayed that this series would have a different outcome. The Cavs had home field advantage but failed to capitalize on it as they allowed the Celtics to split the first two games before heading to Boston for Games Three and Four.

Game Three in Boston turned into the LeBron James spectacular from the opening tip-off as James put on a basketball clinic en route to a thirty-eight-point masterpiece. He could have had well over fifty points but played only thirty-nine minutes because the Cavs were blowing out the Celtics all night long. Antawn Jamison helped out with twenty points, and the game was never close. In the end, Cleveland came out on top, 124–95. The unthinkable was about to occur, but first, the notorious Game Five had to happen.

Chapter 12

The Decision

On paper, LeBron James had every right to leave Cleveland in free agency when his contract expired in the summer of 2010. On paper, it simply stated that he was drafted by the Cavaliers; he never actually chose to play here. On paper, he didn't owe Cleveland anything more than his best effort, which he fully gave during his time there. However, as we all know, life is based on so much more than what is on paper.

James began to feel the pressure of the expiring contract well before Game Four of the Boston series; he had heard it from the fans and media for the previous three years. Everyone wanted to know if he would stay in Cleveland when the contract was up. The bigger question was: would he bring Cleveland fans their long-awaited championship before decision time? So much pressure and so many questions were on the line as the Boston series intensified. Up until this point, the organization and James had done a great job of ignoring the questions and the pressure regarding his possible departure. The focal point always remained the same: to win a championship. But all that would change heading into Game Five of the series.

The Cavs had dropped Game Four a few days earlier, which brought the series back to Cleveland tied at two games apiece. There was a slight chance that if they failed to win, it might be the last time James ever played in Cleveland as a member of the Cavaliers. Many people dismissed the chance of that actually happening, but for the first time ever, it seemed that the immense pressure finally got to James. No one other than those in the locker room truly knows what happened before Game Five of the series, but many rumors have surfaced. Whatever the case may be, LeBron came out flat.

The game started off OK as the Cavaliers led 23–20 at the end of the first quarter. It was in the second quarter that things started to go horribly wrong. Boston outscored the Cavaliers 30–21 and never looked back as the Cavs began to self-destruct. All five starters from Boston scored in the double digits, as did Glen Davis, who came off the bench to score fifteen himself. The Cavs' defensive effort was terrible, and they seemed to sleepwalk through the final three quarters of the game. By the time it was over, they were on the losing end of a 120–88 blowout.

The game will forever be remembered by Cleveland fans as "the Game Five debacle" and "the night LeBron choked." James, who had been one of the best post-season players for several years, had the worst game in his playoff career. He seemed slow and apathetic the entire night. He wasn't his normally aggressive self and passed off many shots instead of driving to the hole. He finished with fifteen points but was only three of fourteen from the field, his worst shooting night as a pro. Shaquille O'Neal did his best to help out with twenty-one points, but it wasn't nearly enough.

With the misery of Game Five still fresh in everyone's minds, the Cavaliers headed back to Boston for Game Six, clinging to hope that LeBron would wake up from his slumber and force a Game Seven. James answered his heavy critics from Game Five and responded with a great effort, scoring twenty-seven points to go along with nineteen rebounds and ten assists. It was another incredible playoff triple-double from James. But it was too little too late, and the red-hot Celtics were not to be stopped. They ended Cleveland's playoff run by closing out Game Six 94–85.

For the second straight year, the Cavaliers had the best record in the East. For the second straight year, they had the league's MVP, LeBron James. And sadly, for the second straight year, they failed to reach the finals. It was clear that James's possible departure from the team made for too large a distraction. In the end, it might have been the Cavs' biggest downfall. Not only did they fail to reach the finals, but also now they had to anguish through the off-season wondering and waiting to see if James would resign. Sadly for the Cavs, LeBron was not about to make things easy on them, as he dragged out his decision to return or leave in free agency.

LeBron James did not take the normal route to free agency, in which the player quietly meets with several teams and then makes his decision. Most of the time, the player's agent or team schedules a press conference and then an announcement is made. Instead of doing the normal, humble thing, James

Byron Scott was called on to lead the new team without LeBron. *Photo by Kenny Roda.*

was talked into having a media circus. There were several big-name free agents available that off-season, and James organized a summit so that they could all get together and discuss their plans. Such a move was unheard of; it reeked of collusion, and it was about to get even worse.

The 2010 free agency class was loaded with big names such as LeBron James, Dwayne Wade, Chris Bosh, Amar'e Stoudemire, Dirk Nowitzki, Carlos Boozer and Joe Johnson, to name a few. Where everyone decided to go would greatly reshape the NBA for a long time to come.

While the free-agent madness was underway, the Cavaliers' front office was in a state of great transition. On June 4, 2010, Danny Ferry left the Cavs of his own accord. He had one month left on his contract. The team had gone 272-138 during his reign as general manager. Head coach Mike Brown had also been fired a few weeks prior, on May 24. Gilbert would later regret the decision and hire him back.

The Cavaliers were attempting to clean house in hopes that LeBron would stay if they brought in a high-profile coach and general manager. They ended up having Chris Grant take over as general manager. Grant was a former vice-president of the Atlanta Hawks and had served under Ferry since coming to Cleveland in 2005. The search for a head coach took a little longer than expected, however, as they failed to lure legendary college coach

Byron Scott meets with the media. *Photo by Kenny Roda.*

Super fan Jennifer Dean meets with new point guard Ramon Sessions. *Courtesy of Jennifer Dean.*

Tom Izzo from Michigan State. Izzo would remain in the college ranks, and the search for a coach would continue elsewhere.

On July 2, 2010, Byron Scott was named head coach of the Cleveland Cavaliers. Scott had an extremely successful career while playing in Los Angles, where he had started on the Showtime Lakers alongside Magic Johnson, James Worthy, Kareem Abdul-Jabbar and A.C. Green. He played for the Lakers for ten consecutive seasons (1983–93) and won three NBA championships (1985, 1987 and 1988). He had a championship pedigree.

When his playing career ended, Scott took over the coaching reins for the New Jersey Nets in 2000–01. The Nets struggled the first season but then caught fire and won fifty-two games the following season. They reached the NBA Finals before losing to Scott's former team, the Los Angeles Lakers. Scott led the Nets right back to the championship round the following season, this time losing to the San Antonio Spurs. Despite the back-to-back finals losses, Scott was able to turn the New Jersey franchise around in a very short amount of time. He was seen as one of the best coaches in the NBA, and that is why it came as shock to everyone when he was fired the following season after a 22-20 start. It was a bizarre move by the Nets' upper management that sent shock waves through the NBA.

Scott would sign on as head coach in New Orleans the following year in hopes of taking the Hornets to the finals. Things did not go well at the start, however, as the team missed the playoffs in each of his first three seasons. In 2007–08 season, the Hornets finally turned it around with star point guard Chris Paul and finished first in the Western Conference Southwest Division. They made it to the conference semifinals before losing to the San Antonio Spurs. They were having their best seasons since moving to New Orleans, and that is why it came as another shock when, nine games into 2009–10 season, Scott was again fired.

The Cavaliers liked what Scott had shown he could do with star players and young superstars in the past, and they hoped he would be the perfect coach to convince LeBron James to remain in Cleveland. One by one, the other free agents made their decisions. Dirk Nowitzki decided to stay in Dallas and resign with the Mavericks; Chris Bosh left Toronto to play for the Heat in Miami, where Dwayne Wade had also just re-signed; Carlos Boozer neglected to come back to Cleveland, instead signing with the Chicago Bulls; and Amar'e Stoudemire elected to leave Phoenix for the New York Knicks. LeBron was the last big free agent remaining.

All that would change on July 10, 2010, when LeBron James put on one of the biggest media spectacles ever seen. Instead of signing a contract and making an announcement with his agent, he decided it would be best to go on national television with infamous sportscaster Jim Gray. The broadcast was aired from the Boys and Girls Club of Greenwich, Connecticut. The show raised $2.5 million for the charity, as well as an additional $3.5 million from advertisement revenue, which was donated to other various charities. ESPN was in charge of airing the media circus and scheduled it for prime time. The program started at 9:00 p.m., but it wasn't until twenty-eight minutes into the show that James finally announced his decision to join fellow all-stars Chris Bosh and Dwayne Wade in Miami. His exact words were as follows:

> In this fall...this is very tough...in this fall, I'm going to take my talents to South Beach and join the Miami Heat. I feel like it's going to give me the best opportunity to win and to win for multiple years, and not only just to win in the regular season or just to win five games in a row or three games in a row—I want to be able to win championships. And I feel like I can compete down there.

The television program drew high ratings, with Nielsen announcing that an average of 9.948 million people watched the show in the United States, with 13.1 million watching at the time of James's announcement.

One thing that drew instant criticism was the phrase "taking my talents to South Beach." Instead of being humble and mentioning the city and team by name, he used a sentence with "my talents" and referred to Miami as "South Beach." That one remark showed his immaturity and selfishness. He didn't need to stay in Cleveland, and he had every right to leave, but it was how he went about it that upset everyone watching. You do not go on national television and embarrass your hometown the way he did. It was this kind of horrendous act that set Cleveland fans ablaze in anger and also made James one of the most hated men in sports.

Cleveland fans instantly revolted against James and could be seen burning replicas of his jersey in the streets. James was later quoted as saying that the whole ordeal might have been a mistake on his part, but he stood by his decision. On September 29, 2010, when asked by Soledad O'Brien of CNN if race was a factor in the fallout from what had become know as "The Decision," James said, "I think so, at times. There's always—you know, a race factor." For many, it was mind-blowing to many that James would pull the race card in such a situation. Color had nothing to do with it; the only color the Cavaliers fans saw was red in anger. Jim Brown had pulled the same race card years earlier to get Paul Brown fired.

James's move to join two fellow all-stars in Miami was also criticized by former greats of the NBA. It had never been done before, and it had everyone in an uproar. Michael Jordan stated that he would not have contacted his rivals from other teams like Magic Johnson and Larry Bird to play on one team together. Jordan stated, "I wanted to defeat those guys." He added that "things are different now. I can't say that's a bad thing. It's an opportunity these kids have today."

Neither LeBron James nor his agents had the courtesy to contact anyone from the Cleveland Cavaliers organization to notify them of their decision. Owner Dan Gilbert did not hesitate to vent his frustration at the situation in an effort to comfort the fans with a solid vote of confidence. Gilbert penned the following letter (in Comic Sans, no less), which was sent out via social media in a matter of minutes following the decision:

Dear Cleveland, All of Northeast Ohio and Cleveland Cavaliers Supporters Wherever You May Be Tonight:

As you now know, our former hero, who grew up in the very region that he deserted this evening, is no longer a Cleveland Cavalier.

This was announced with a several-day, narcissistic, self-promotional build-up culminating with a national TV special of his "decision" unlike anything ever "witnessed" in the history of sports and probably the history of entertainment.

Clearly, this is bitterly disappointing to all of us.

The good news is that the ownership, team, and the rest of the hard-working, loyal, and driven staff over here at your hometown Cavaliers have not betrayed you nor NEVER will betray you.

There is so much more to tell you about the events of the recent past and our more than exciting future. Over the next several days and weeks, we will be communicating much of that to you.

You simply don't deserve this kind of cowardly betrayal.

You have given so much and deserve so much more.

In the meantime, I want to make one statement to you tonight:

"I PERSONALLY GUARANTEE THAT THE CLEVELAND CAVALIERS WILL WIN AN NBA CHAMPIONSHIP BEFORE THE SELF-TITLED FORMER 'KING' WINS ONE."

You can take it to the bank.

If you thought we were motivated before tonight to bring the hardware to Cleveland, I can tell you that this shameful display of selfishness and betrayal by one of our very own has shifted our "motivation" to previously unknown and previously never experienced levels. Some people think they should go to heaven but NOT have to die to get there. Sorry, but that's simply not how it works.

This shocking act of disloyalty from our homegrown "chosen one" sends the exact opposite lesson of what we would want our children to learn. And "who" we would want them to grow-up to become.

But the good news is that this heartless and callous action can only serve as the antidote to the so-called "curse" on Cleveland, Ohio.

The self-declared former "king" will be taking the "curse" with him down south. And until he does "right" by Cleveland and Ohio, James (and the town where he plays) will unfortunately own this dreaded spell and bad karma.

Just watch.

Sleep well, Cleveland.

Tomorrow is a new and much brighter day....

I PROMISE you that our energy, focus, capital, knowledge and experience will be directed at one thing and one thing only: DELIVERING YOU the championship you have long deserved and is long overdue.

Dan Gilbert
Majority Owner
Cleveland Cavaliers

It was comforting to Cleveland fans that the owner would show such confidence in the team and city. He showed that he was willing to stick up for Cleveland and its die-hard fans. The city was in pain, and with an arrogant local sports talk host constantly putting the city down and laughing at Cleveland, it was nice to see a man with the power of Gilbert fight on behalf of the city. And that is more than just a mile-high statement.

Mary Schmitt Boyer gives her opinion on how the entire spectacle was handled:

He [James] had the right to do what he did, but the way he handled it was incorrect. If he had it to do over again, I don't think he would have handled it the way he did. He was young, and I don't know if he got bad advice or what his reasoning was. It could have been handled in a much better way. He could have said that he had given Cleveland what he could for seven years and it was time, but he didn't. I just think there was a way to exit with far less fanfare. Part of me thinks that he had never been away from home, as opposed to kids who go away for college, and I think at that age that maybe he felt it was time to try something else. I don't think he had animosity towards the city of Cleveland. I just think he thought it was time to try something else. He had given Cleveland seven marvelous years and lit the city up like Vegas, much like he promised he would. I know there are still people who will never forgive him for what he did. He could have done it in a different way.

Suddenly without their best player, the Cavaliers needed to do everything possible to recover from such an epic loss. The problem was that the free-agency season was pretty much over, as LeBron was the last big name to sign. Cleveland traded away Delonte West, who had had a rough season both on and off the court, and Sebastian Telfair to the Minnesota Timberwolves for Ryan Hollins and Ramon Sessions. They also signed backup point guard Manny Harris before the season began.

On Wednesday, October 27, 2010, the Cavaliers took the court without their star player for the first time in seven years. It was a feeling of great uncertainty and anxiety, but most felt they were still a good team without James. They were also without all-star point guard Mo Williams, who was out the entire first week of the season due to an injury. It looked to be a long night as the defending Eastern Conference champion Boston Celtics were in town to the open the season.

Not only were they missing James and Williams, but they were also without their center from the previous year. Shaquille O'Neal had also left in free agency and was now a member of the visiting Boston Celtics. Additionally, Zydrunas Ilgauskas had followed James to Miami in free agency. With West, James, Williams, Ilgauskas and O'Neal all missing from the previous year's starting lineup, the Cavs were forced to field a much different starting five. The backcourt featured Anthony Parker and Ramon Sessions, while the frontcourt boasted Anderson Varejao, J.J. Hickson and Jamario Moon.

It was a giant mismatch on paper, but Cleveland stood a fighting chance in front of a home sellout crowd of 20,562 rabid fans. They were hurt, and they needed a win to give them hope that the season might not be that bad after all. Playing in their favor was the fact that the Boston Celtics had

had an emotional night themselves the previous evening, as they were fresh off an opening-night win against LeBron James and the Miami Heat. The chance that Boston might have a letdown against the Cavs was strong.

Cleveland played Boston hard through the first three quarters and trailed only 73–68 heading into the decisive fourth quarter. The Cavaliers used the strength of the loud fans and rebounded from a hostile off-season to mount a courageous fourth-quarter comeback. They played inspired defense and held the Celtics to just fourteen fourth-quarter points. Thanks to a furious rally that saw the Cavs score twenty-seven points of their own, they walked out of Quicken Loans Arena with a 95–87 opening-night win. The defense was so impressive that it held Paul Pierce to only thirteen points and Kevin Garnett to only nine.

The Cavs received a surprisingly explosive opening-night effort out of second-year sensation JJ Hickson, who led all scorers with twenty-one points. Also chipping in with sixteen off the bench was Boobie Gibson. Ramon Sessions made the most out of his first game with the Cavaliers, adding fourteen points of his own. It was a great first night that proved that life would go on without the so-called chosen one.

The Cavaliers stumbled a bit after the opening-night win, finishing November with a record of 7-10. It wasn't great by any stretch, but it was far better than anyone thought possible. It was at that point, however, that things started going downhill quickly. They got caught up in a ten-game losing streak that was snapped only by a nail-biting overtime win against the New York Knicks at home. It was after the win against the Knicks, however, that things started to spiral completely out of control as they went on a NBA-record twenty-six-game losing streak. From December 18, 2010, through February 9, 2011, the Cavs did not win a single game. It was mortifying to go through such a horrendous stretch.

Five days after the epic losing streak came to an end, the highly powered Los Angeles Lakers rolled into town. They had won the NBA championship in the two previous seasons and were looking great again this season. The Cavaliers came into the contest with a record of 9-46, and few people, if any, gave them a chance. The Cavs once again flourished in the underdog role and jumped out to an early lead against the Lakers. They managed to hold on to the lead all night and swipe the 104–99 upset win. It was the perfect way to head into the All-Star Break.

A few weeks after the All-Star Break, the Cavaliers made a trade that would change the course of team history for a very long time to come. On February 24, 2011, they traded Jamario Moon and Mo Williams to the Los

Angeles Clippers for Baron Davis and a 2011 first-round draft pick. Davis did not do too much during his short time in Cleveland; however, the draft pick would come up large only a few short months later.

The Cavs were struggling with all the changes, and they held a paltry 14-58 record as LeBron James and the high-powered Miami Heat came to town on March 29, 2011. After a dead-even first quarter, Cleveland exploded in the second quarter and had a surprising nine-point lead heading into halftime. The fans were loud all game and hoped that they could get the last laugh against LeBron with an upset win.

James brought his very best once again and finished with a triple-double (twenty-seven points, ten rebounds and twelve assists). But the Cavaliers never stopped believing they could pull off the upset, and in the end, they did exactly that. When the last second ran off the clock, the Cavs had pulled off the 102–90 upset win. It was a major statement and a feel-good moment for a city and franchise that had had to live with so much pain during the previous ten months.

The Cavaliers won only four more games after that fateful night against Miami, including their last two of the season to finish with a 19-63 record. But it was big wins against the likes of the Knicks, Celtics, Lakers, Clippers and Heat that showed just how much fighting spirit the city and team still had left. Despite the rough season, their luck was about to change drastically, as they were about to send a young man with his bow tie to play the lottery.

Chapter 13

The Lotto Winners

One of the few advantages of having a bad record in the NBA is that it allows your team to have more ping-pong balls in the annual draft lottery. Unlike other leagues, the NBA decides who will receive the top three picks in its draft based on a blind lottery of the teams that did not make the playoffs that season. The worse your record is, the more ping-pong balls you get placed into the lottery.

Overall, the 2011 draft was seen as being weak. The top two players were Kyrie Irving out of Duke University and Derrick Williams out of the University of Arizona. They were the cream of the crop, the two players who all teams wanted to secure in the upcoming June draft.

The lottery was held on May 17, 2011, in Secaucus, New Jersey. The Cavaliers sent a contingent of hometown favorites such as Bernie Kosar and other luminaries to root on Nick Gilbert, the young son of owner Dan Gilbert. Nick was dressed sharply and sporting his lucky bow tie. The Cavaliers had a 22.7 percent chance to win, combining the 19.9 percent chance from their own pick and the 2.8 percent chance from the Clippers' pick, which Cleveland acquired in the Mo Williams deal.

As each team came off the board and its name was announced, the Cavaliers remained on the board, and the hopes of the bewildered Cleveland fans began to increase. The commercial break in the program came with only three teams left with a chance to win; the Cavaliers were one of them. The third pick went to the Utah Jazz, which left the Minnesota Timberwolves and Cleveland Cavaliers as the two remaining teams. After everything the Cavs and

Above: Tyler Zeller during warm-ups. *Photo by Sam Bourquin.*

Left: Kyrie Irving meets with the press. *Photo by Kenny Roda.*

Opposite: Kyrie Irving at Media Day 2012. *Photo by Kenny Roda.*

their fans had been through, it almost seemed like poetic justice when the second-place card was opened and it read, "Minnesota Timberwolves." After a year of suffering, the Cavaliers had just won the lottery.

For the first time in a long while, basketball fans in Cleveland had a reason to cheer. General manager Chris Grant would have his work cut out for him, however, because unlike in 2003, the first pick was not a sure thing. The Cavs would really have to do their homework this time around and make sure not to blow the pick. It was crucial to get it right because the team needed a fresh start, and they needed a superstar to make that happen.

The 2011 NBA draft was held on June 23, 2011, at the Prudential Center in Newark, New Jersey. After much research and debate, the Cavaliers selected Kyrie Irving, point guard out of Duke University. Irving had led the Blue Devils in scoring with 17.4 points per game on 53.2 percent shooting through the first eight games of the season. He wasn't just good at scoring, however, as he also averaged 5.1 assists, 3.8 rebounds and 1.5 steals per game. The problem was that he had played in only eight games before getting hurt. Irving suffered a severe ligament injury in his right big toe that sidelined him for the remainder of the regular season. He was able to return for the post-season NCAA tournament in March, helping Duke reach the Sweet Sixteen. The Blue Devils eventually lost to Arizona, but Irving exploded for 28.0 points in the contest.

The Cavaliers also owned the fourth pick in the draft and selected power forward Tristan Thompson out of the University of Texas. Like Irving, who was born in Australia, Thompson was also born outside of the United States. He was born in Toronto, Ontario, and raised in Brampton. Thompson was a physical power forward, standing at six feet, nine inches and weighing in at

Dion Waters is a solid number-two guard. *Photo by Kenny Roda.*

Kenny Roda speaks with Tristan Thompson. *Photo by Kenny Roda.*

238 pounds. He was the presence down low that the Cavaliers sorely needed as they had been lacking one for very long.

The NBA and Cleveland would both have to wait a little longer than expected to see Irving make his debut because, once again, the NBA owners and players were mired in another work stoppage. Some in the media believed that the dispute between the owners and players was so strong that the entire season might be canceled. After months of dispute, a resolution was finally reached, and the season was set to open up on December 26, 2011.

Thirty games into the season, the young Cavaliers were hanging tough with a 13-17 record. They were doing much better than many expected, and that gave hope to the fans for the second half of the season. Both Irving and his teammate Thompson were named to the 2012 Rising Stars Challenge. Irving played for Team Chuck, while Thompson played for Team Shaq. Irving scored thirty-four points in the game, earning MVP honors. It was his first chance to showcase his talents in front of a national audience, and he didn't disappoint.

The Cavaliers tired out down the stretch and suffered losing streaks of six and nine games. They were 0-5 in overtime games, which was something that Byron Scott would have to really work on with his young team in the future. They finished 21-45 in a strike-shortened season, an improvement from the year before. What was even more promising, however, was the play of their young superstar Irving.

Kyrie Irving won the 2012 NBA Rookie of the Year Award, receiving 117 of a possible 120 first-place votes. He was also selected to the NBA All-Rookie First Team. Irving averaged 18.5 points with 5.4 assists. These were especially impressive numbers for the rookie considering he missed fifteen games due to injury.

Thompson also impressed critics, as he was voted to the NBA All-Rookie Second Team. Thompson came off the bench behind veteran forwards Antawn Jamison and Anderson Varejao for the first three months of his rookie season but still managed to make his presence known on both ends of the floor. His production increased in February as his minutes increased, and he recorded three double-doubles that month. He was later inserted into the starting lineup, and it appears he will remain there for a long time to come.

The Cavs would once again own two of the top twenty picks in the first round of the 2012 draft. With Kyrie Irving and Tristan Thompson both coming off of strong rookie seasons, it was crucial to continue adding key pieces to the talented nucleus. With the fourth overall pick in the draft, they selected Dion Waiters from Syracuse. He was strong off the bench and was one of the top sixth men in the Big East Conference. In the 2010–11 NCAA tournament, Waiters scored 18 points off the bench in a second-round loss to Marquette. He continued to be one of the best sixth men in college basketball during his sophomore season, averaging 12.6 points, 2.5 assists and 2.3 rebounds per game. In addition to being selected to the All-Big East Tournament team, he was also named the Big East Sixth Man of the Year and an AP Honorable Mention All-American.

Waiters's main goal in the NBA would be to provide a solid one-two punch with Kyrie Irving. Many NBA experts thought that if the two could learn how to coexist, the Cavaliers would possess one of the strongest backcourts in the Eastern Conference.

With their second first-round pick, the Cavs made a trade for the draft rights of center Tyler Zeller out of the University of North Carolina. Zeller had been voted Indiana Mr. Basketball in 2008 before leaving for college and would be the perfect fit at center, as he stood an impressive seven feet tall. Zeller was a four-year player at UNC and had improved drastically each season, averaging 16.5 points per game on 55.3 percent shooting during his senior year. Zeller was voted to the All-ACC First Team his senior year and was named the ACC Player of the Year, both of which were huge honors. When he was selected as the seventeenth overall pick, he became the fourth Tar Heel to be selected in the first round.

Expectations were high heading into the 2012–13 season. Unfortunately for the Cavaliers, however, the season was riddled with injuries to their key players, and they finished with only twenty-four wins. Kyrie Irving missed twenty-three games due to injury but was still impressive enough to be voted to the Eastern Conference All-Star team. He had a great All-Star Weekend, including walking away with the Three-Point Shootout championship trophy.

Kyrie Irving led the team in scoring by averaging 22.5 points a game. He also led the team in assists by averaging 5.9 a game. He was quickly becoming one of the elite players in the NBA.

Dion Waiters also missed twenty-one games due to injury but was able to impress when he was on the court. He averaged 14.7 points, 3 assists and 1 steal per game. Waiters was selected to play in the NBA Rising Stars game during All-Star Weekend along with teammates Kyrie Irving, Tristan Thompson and Tyler Zeller. Waiters came off of the bench to score 23 points for Shaquille O'Neal's team. He had a career-high 33 points on January 14 against the Sacramento Kings. Despite the injuries, it was a promising first season for Waiters.

The Cavaliers decided to part ways with Byron Scott after only three seasons and bring back beloved former head coach Mike Brown. They believed Brown would be the perfect man to lead this new and highly talented set of superstars to the promised land. In addition to having several talented young guns on the roster, the kid with the magic bow tie was headed back to the lottery!

Chapter 14

The Future Is Now

The Cavaliers have gone through several ups and downs in their history but have always managed to bounce back and electrify the crowds. The 2013–14 season was just one more reminder of the resolve of the entire Cavaliers organization. Things started off very well, as it was once again Nick Gilbert and his lucky bow tie winning the draft lottery. It was the second time in three years the Cavaliers were granted the first overall pick in the draft.

The Cavaliers used the pick to select Anthony Bennett out of UNLV. Bennett started as a freshman and made an immediate impact at power forward. He averaged 16.1 points and 8.1 rebounds a game. He was also efficient with his shooting, going 53.3 percent from the field overall and 37.5 percent from 3-point range. He was a presence on the boards and a dangerous outside shooter for a man of his impressive stature. Bennett would be counted on by the Cavaliers to play small forward. They believed he would mesh well with other recent draft picks Zeller, Waiters, Thompson and Irving. They had the potential to be the starting five of the future.

The Cavs also made two key moves in free agency, one that would pay off and another that simply did not. They brought in Jarrett Jack, a veteran guard who could play well off the bench when called on. They also signed Andrew Bynum to a low-risk, high-reward deal. Bynum had been a force on the Lakers in previous years when he was able to stay healthy. The move came with mild risk, as the contract was very team friendly just in case the big man didn't pan out.

The season once again had its up and downs, including seven overtime games by the All-Star Break. Speaking of the All-Star Game, it was dominated by game MVP Kyrie Irving, who put on a show for the entire NBA and represented Cleveland extremely well in the process. Irving was on fire and led the Eastern Conference to a win with thirty-one points and fourteen assists.

Kyrie Irving and Dion Waiters were getting stronger by the night. It was clear that when Irving and Waiters were both healthy, the Cavaliers possessed one of the most talented backcourts in the NBA.

Another key addition was the move to deal away the selfish and lazy Andrew Bynum, who had done nothing but cause trouble since coming to town, and bring in Luol Deng. The Cavaliers traded Andrew Bynum, a 2014 first-round draft pick, a 2015 second-round draft pick and a 2016 second-round draft pick to the Chicago Bulls for Luol Deng. Chicago has the option to swap first-round picks with Cleveland in 2015 if Cleveland's selection is within the fifteen-to-thirty range. Deng was seen as a hardworking team player and someone who could make the players around him better—the exact opposite of what they were getting from Bynum.

It was a great move by general manager Chris Grant to deal Bynum for Deng. However, it would be his last move as general manager, as he was fired by the Cavaliers on February 6, 2014. The Cavs needed a spark, and Grant was seen as the fall guy. He was replaced with David Griffin. The immediate impact of the move was felt as the Cavaliers won six straight games following the switch at GM.

David Griffin wasted no time making his first move. On February 20, 2014, he traded Earl Clark, Henry Sims and two second-round draft picks to the Philadelphia 76ers for Spencer Hawes. It was a move to solidify the frontcourt as often-injured Anderson Varejao could no longer be counted on to carry heavy minutes. Hawes was a beast on the boards and could add the immediate physical presence the Cavs needed.

For the first time in four seasons, the Cavaliers remained in the playoff hunt with only a week to go in the season. They narrowly missed the playoffs in the end, but they did improve on their previous season's record by winning nine more games.

With young, extremely talented players such as Kyrie Irving, Anthony Bennett, Tristan Thompson, Dion Waiters and Tyler Zeller, the Cavs will be a force to be reckoned with for many years to come. It is crystal clear that the proper nucleus is in place, and it is only a matter of time before the Cleveland Cavaliers are once again battling for an NBA championship!

And now that young nucleus will once again have a new coach in charge. Mike Brown could not rekindle the magic he once had, and GM David Griffin decided to fire him at the close of the 2012–13 season. Griffin felt that the team needed an offensive-minded coach who could inspire the Cavaliers to play more like the Wilkens-led teams of the 1980s and early '90s. He interviewed several candidates—including former players Mark Price, Tyron Lue and Alvin Gentry—before finding his man in David Blatt. Blatt, born and raised in Massachusetts, played his college basketball for Hall of Famer Pete Carill at Princeton before embarking on a hugely successful head coaching career overseas. A coaching icon in the Euroleague for many years, Blatt was offered a reported four-year deal worth a whopping $20 million to come coach the Cavs. He is the first coach to make the leap from Europe to the NBA as a head coach. Blatt coached undermanned Macabbi Tel Aviv to a dramatic upset victory over Real Madrid in the Euroleague championships in 2014. He has had tremendous success during his two decades overseas, winning the 2007 EuroBasket championship with Russia and a bronze medal in the 2012 Summer Olympics in London.

The Cavs' incredible draft lottery luck continued in 2014 as they won once again. They have now won it three times in the past four years, the first team to ever achieve such a remarkable feat. There was plenty from which to pick in the 2014 draft, including Andrew Wiggins, a six-foot-eight forward out of Kansas, and his teammate Joel Embiid, a seven-foot center whom many considered the top pick until a week before the draft, when he hurt his foot and had to undergo emergency surgery. The expected choice was Jabari Parker, a six-foot-eight small forward who was considered the most NBA-ready. There were also rumors running rampant that LeBron would opt out of his contract with Miami and come home. No one knew what would happen until Thursday night, June 26, when Cleveland chose Andrew Wiggins.

Chapter 15

The King Comes Home

There were rumblings as far back as 2012 about LeBron James, who had an opt-out option in his contract, eventually coming back to Cleveland after the 2014 season. As the Miami Heat were getting crushed in the 2014 NBA Finals by the San Antonio Spurs, those small rumblings of a return started to heat up. Suddenly, with the way the Heat were crumbling in the NBA Finals, it didn't seem like such a long shot that LeBron would return.

As the Heat were losing in the finals, the Cavaliers were starting to gain steam. They were awarded the number-one pick in the upcoming draft and convinced European coaching legend David Blatt to travel across the pond and become their new coach. General manager David Griffin worked hard to secure a max contract extension with Kyrie Irving, paying him $90 million over five years. The Cavaliers had locked up their best player for a long time to come, and this spoke volumes of the positive direction in which the team was headed.

Meanwhile, back in San Antonio, the Spurs were putting the finishing touches on a 4–1 series win, just in time to end Fathers' Day on a happy note for men across America rooting against LeBron James. The Spurs won big to close the series, averaging an eighteen-point differential per victory, the largest such margin in NBA Finals history. James was upset and didn't even play the last six minutes of the series clincher. You could sense it in the air—the fate of the NBA was about to change.

When asked in the post-series press conference about his plans for the off-season and whether he would opt out of his contract early, James was very noncommittal and simply stated that he needed to spend time with his family. He wasn't tipping his cards, although most of the media felt strongly that James would stay in Miami.

As the off-season frenzy began, the odds of LeBron staying in Miami remained strong. What the national media couldn't control, however, was the fairy tale starting to take shape. LeBron James's wife was the first to hint that a possible return was in the works when she sent out a message on her Instagram account that read, "Home Sweet Home—the countdown is real!" It was attached to a picture of Ohio with a heart placed over Akron, James's hometown. It was the first indicator that maybe, just maybe, LeBron was coming home. Not long afterward, it was confirmed that Savannah James was pregnant with the couple's third child. The rumors continued to go wild when it was announced that LeBron had enrolled his sons into the Bath school system. It was the glimmer of hope that Cavalier fans needed to once again believe it was possible.

Things continued to look more and more hopeful when LeBron James opted out of his contract days before he had to. This didn't mean that his days in Miami were done just yet, but it did mean that James could now sign with any team he wanted. His fellow teammates Dwayne Wade and Chris Bosh also opted out. The thought was that they would all take smaller contracts so that GM Pat Riley would have the cap space to build around them, perhaps with fellow free-agent All Star Carmelo Anthony. Many believed that the Heat were simply retooling for yet another run at the title. The fans of Cleveland, however, did not give up hope.

LeBron James continued to show his maturity and this time did everything the right way. He spent time with his family and allowed everything to cool off. He did not hold another media spectacle; instead, he let his agent, Rich Paul of LRMR, handle it privately with only a few teams. It was soon revealed that James had only two serious options: Cleveland and Miami. The drama was about to explode off the charts!

With the world watching and everyone claiming to have their sources, LeBron Watch 2.0 began to hit its full stride. Miami Heat general manager Pat Riley did not help his own cause when he stated that the Big Three needed to stay together to finish what they had started. If anything, that played more into LeBron's decision to come back home, as many had stated for years that he had unfinished business in Cleveland to attend to.

The longer LeBron went without re-signing with the Heat, the more and more people started to believe that King James might be coming back home to Cleveland. The hysteria hit an all-time high on Sunday night, July 6, when Dan Gilbert's private jet was spotted flying to South Beach. The rumor mill ran rampant with speculation that Gilbert was there to talk James into coming back. At first, the rumors were denied, but it was later learned that Gilbert had indeed visited LeBron. In a July 11 interview with Yahoo Sports' Adrian Wojnarowski, Gilbert talked about the meeting and why it was so important for him to apologize for his letter after James left in 2010. Gilbert explained, "We had five great years together and one terrible night. I told him how sorry I was, expressed regret for how that night went and how I let all the emotion and passion for the situation carry me away. I told him I wish I had never done it, that I wish I could take it back." It took a lot of guts and humbleness from Gilbert to admit that he had reacted too harshly in the heat of the moment. James told Gilbert that he also wished he had handled it differently and that they both made mistakes from which they needed to move on. James was angry with himself for "The Decision" and how he handled it. It was a breakthrough moment for James and Gilbert, and for the first time in four years, peace was on its way to being achieved.

Dan Gilbert felt awful about the letter and said that he didn't want that to be the thing that defined him. He was sure to give credit to the management team of James, Maverick Carter and Rich Paul. They made Gilbert feel comfortable and initiated a sense of peace in the air during a stressful situation. Gilbert described them as being "so professional with us through the whole process." The meeting with Gilbert and LeBron showed the power of forgiveness. Even if James never came back to Cleveland, it was a moment that needed to happen. Both men needed to clear the air for the ease of their own souls. Gilbert left that day with no deal in place, but he and James had done something more important than dollars and numbers—they had lifted the heavy weight on their souls and in their hearts. No matter what happened next, it was a healing they both needed.

Dan Gilbert went on to tell Adrian Wojnarowski:

Do a Google search on me, and it's the first thing that comes up. To a certain segment of society, it's like somebody killed somebody, like somebody killed their kid. I told LeBron, "That letter didn't hurt anybody more than it hurt me." For the first two months, I kept thousands of letters—not hundreds—thousands written to me. There were 90-year-old ladies and CEOs, and I realized that that letter had transcended the event; it went far beyond LeBron. After a few months, I would re-read it and just be full of regret. That wasn't me—that wasn't who I am. I didn't mean most of the things I said in there. The venom it produced, from all sides…I wish…I wish I had never done it.

For Gilbert to come out and admit this showed true class and the fact that even a billionaire can admit a mistake. It is a lesson from which all of America could learn. The peace achieved between James and Gilbert proves that no problem between two people is too big to be overcome. Two men with all the fame and money in the world seeking forgiveness from each other in search of peace—it is a message that can bring tears to the eyes of grown men.

So, the week of madness began early on Monday morning with both local and national reporters confirming that it was indeed Dan Gilbert's private jet that had flown down to meet with James. The drama would move from South Beach to Las Vegas, as James's Skill Camp was about to begin. Some of the top amateur athletes in the world assembled in Vegas for the camp. As that was going on, every media outlet in the world was trying to squeeze any clue possible out of LeBron in regards to where he was going. The national guys were slowly cracking and giving Cleveland at least a puncher's chance to get the king back.

Twitter was on fire. Local Cleveland basketball reporter Sam Amico picked up over twenty-five thousand extra followers in a matter of hours, as everybody was desperate for information. People started to hang on every tweet from anyone in the know. It got to the point that every sports radio show in Miami and Cleveland transitioned to 100 percent LeBron coverage. Everyone had a theory and a source, and the frenzy ultimately reached a level even greater than that of 2010.

Chris Bosh was offered a four-year, $88 million deal with the Houston Rockets but refused to give them an answer because he wanted to see what his teammate and friend LeBron James would do first. It was unprecedented for an athlete to put that kind of money on hold because he was too hung up on what someone else was going to do.

Carmelo Anthony was being recruited heavily by both the New York Knicks and Los Angeles Lakers, but even the hype behind Anthony paled in comparison to the insane amount of press and extremely personal coverage LeBron James was getting. It got to the point that every single move James made was being reported on Twitter. The hype was real, the pulse of Cleveland was raging and the fans stayed up all night in anticipation of an announcement. It had gotten to the point that even national media members such as Chris Broussard, Chris Sheridan and Stephen A. Smith started to believe and report that Cleveland was a serious contender.

The Cavaliers continued to apply the pressure and show James they were for real when they pulled off a trade with the Nets and Celtics that cleared up over $20 million in cap room. They dealt Tyler Zeller, Jarrett Jack and Sergey Karasev as part of the move. The cap room was made to bring in LeBron James and sign him to a max contract.

Pat Riley sensed that James and his dream team were slipping away and called for an emergency meeting at LeBron's camp in Las Vegas on Wednesday, July 9, to meet with James and try to talk him into to re-signing with the Heat. Riley pitched James hard on the idea that, despite having only two returning players on the roster, the Heat had the funds available to bring James back with a max contract and still be able to sign Bosh and Wade for smaller deals, allowing them to bring in other talent as well. Riley had already picked up Danny Granger and Josh McRoberts in free agency, planned on signing Bosh and Wade and had already drafted James's favorite college point guard, Shabazz Napier, from the National Champion UConn Huskies. This was crucial because James made it known during the NCAA tournament that he had a special affinity for Napier, calling him the best player in the tournament. It was a move strictly to appeal to James.

Riley left Vegas on that fateful Wednesday night cocky as ever but without a deal in place. Although he would never admit it, Riley had to be nervous. He had given his best pitch to James, but it wasn't enough to get him to sign. And although everyone thought that James would make his decision shortly after the meeting with Riley, he did not. The newest rumor was that James would make it on his website sometime the following day after speaking with his family.

As Thursday morning, July 10, began, the sports world stood still as it waited on word from the king regarding his next move. Word broke out that someone in James's camp had asked the Bath Township police department to surround his house between the hours of 3:00 p.m. and 11:00 p.m. Another rumor quickly broke out that he would make his decision known at 3:30 p.m., which only fueled the excitement because 330 is the area code for Akron. People knew of James's love of Akron; he even has a "330" tattoo on his right forearm. Like most of the rumors and so-called sources, this story turned out to be false as well. However, it didn't stop fans from swarming his house and waiting outside the gates seemingly ready to erupt with jubilation at a moment's notice. At one point, a couple high school girls set up a lemonade stand and ice cream stand. Random people were parking in the middle of the street, getting out of their cars and taking "selfies." It was nuts, and yet the wait dragged on.

Evening turned into night, and the decision still hadn't been made. LeBron had wrapped up his skills camp in Vegas and was headed back to Miami.

He was spotted with Wade on his trip back, and many felt this was the kiss of death for Cleveland. It was later revealed that Wade himself wasn't even aware of the decision at that point. Everyone went to bed late Thursday night/Friday morning still not knowing.

ESPN NBA reporter Chris Broussard appeared on *Mike & Mike in the Morning* early on Friday, July 11, to talk about the incredible drama that was going on. He claimed that James would have already returned to Cleveland if he weren't still hung up on the letter from Gilbert. Broussard was way out of line, and many people who read his article following the appearance were irate with him.

As the morning dragged into the early afternoon, it finally happened. LeBron James had made his decision—the king was coming home! He revealed his decision in an "essay" to SI reporter Lee Jenkins and posted it on SI.com. His emotional essay to the fans read as follows:

> *Before anyone ever cared where I would play basketball, I was a kid from Northeast Ohio. It's where I walked. It's where I ran. It's where I cried. It's where I bled. It holds a special place in my heart. People there have seen me grow up. I sometimes feel like I'm their son. Their passion can be overwhelming. But it drives me. I want to give them hope when I can. I want to inspire them when I can. My relationship with Northeast Ohio is bigger than basketball. I didn't realize that four years ago. I do now.*
>
> *Remember when I was sitting up there at the Boys & Girls Club in 2010? I was thinking, "This is really tough." I could feel it. I was leaving something I had spent a long time creating. If I had to do it all over again, I'd obviously do things differently, but I'd still have left. Miami, for me, has been almost like college for other kids. These past four years helped raise me into who I am. I became a better player and a better man. I learned from a franchise that had been where I wanted to go. I will always think of Miami as my second home. Without the experiences I had there, I wouldn't be able to do what I'm doing today.*
>
> *I went to Miami because of D-Wade and CB. We made sacrifices to keep UD. I loved becoming a big bro to Rio. I believed we could do something magical if we came together. And that's exactly what we did! The hardest thing to leave is what I built with those guys. I've talked to some of them and will talk to others. Nothing will ever change what we accomplished. We are brothers for life. I also want to thank Micky Arison and Pat Riley for giving me an amazing four years.*

I'm doing this essay because I want an opportunity to explain myself uninterrupted. I don't want anyone thinking: "He and Erik Spoelstra didn't get along."…"He and Riles didn't get along."…"The Heat couldn't put the right team together." That's absolutely not true.

I'm not having a press conference or a party. After this, it's time to get to work.

When I left Cleveland, I was on a mission. I was seeking championships, and we won two. But Miami already knew that feeling. Our city hasn't had that feeling in a long, long, long time. My goal is still to win as many titles as possible, no question. But what's most important for me is bringing one trophy back to Northeast Ohio.

I always believed that I'd return to Cleveland and finish my career there. I just didn't know when. After the season, free agency wasn't even a thought. But I have two boys, and my wife, Savannah, is pregnant with a girl. I started thinking about what it would be like to raise my family in my hometown. I looked at other teams, but I wasn't going to leave Miami for anywhere except Cleveland. The more time passed, the more it felt right. This is what makes me happy.

To make the move I needed the support of my wife and my mom, who can be very tough. The letter from Dan Gilbert, the booing of the Cleveland fans, the jerseys being burned—seeing all that was hard for them. My emotions were more mixed. It was easy to say, "OK, I don't want to deal with these people ever again." But then you think about the other side. What if I were a kid who looked up to an athlete, and that athlete made me want to do better in my own life, and then he left? How would I react? I've met with Dan, face-to-face, man-to-man. We've talked it out. Everybody makes mistakes. I've made mistakes as well. Who am I to hold a grudge?

I'm not promising a championship. I know how hard that is to deliver. We're not ready right now. No way. Of course, I want to win next year, but I'm realistic. It will be a long process, much longer than it was in 2010. My patience will get tested. I know that. I'm going into a situation with a young team and a new coach. I will be the old head. But I get a thrill out of bringing a group together and helping them reach a place they didn't know they could go. I see myself as a mentor now, and I'm excited to lead some of these talented young guys. I think I can help Kyrie Irving become one of the best point guards in our league. I think I can help elevate Tristan Thompson and Dion Waiters. And I can't wait to reunite with Anderson Varejao, one of my favorite teammates.

But this is not about the roster or the organization. I feel my calling here goes above basketball. I have a responsibility to lead, in more ways than one, and I take that very seriously. My presence can make a difference in Miami, but I think it can mean more where I'm from. I want kids in Northeast Ohio, like the hundreds of Akron third-graders I sponsor through my foundation, to realize that there's no better place to grow up. Maybe some of them will come home after college and start a family or open a business. That would make me smile. Our community, which has struggled so much, needs all the talent it can get.

In Northeast Ohio, nothing is given. Everything is earned. You work for what you have.

I'm ready to accept the challenge. I'm coming home.

The essay from James was pure class and brought a tear to the eye of every person from Northeast Ohio who read it. It was real, it was honest, it was humble and it was exactly what he needed to say to get full forgiveness and redemption. Cleveland was ready to forgive, and the approach James took made it ten times easier. The chosen one had come home! This proved how much he had matured and that going to Miami had made him a man. It showed him how to lead, and he is coming back to a better roster now than what he left behind in 2010. The glory days are here once more, and the Cleveland Cavaliers are once again the talk of the sports world!

Epilogue

Over the course of their rich history, the Cleveland Cavaliers have shown the ability to rise from the ashes and become conference contenders numerous times. No matter the odds or player personnel, they have used the never-say-die attitude of the city and provided countless thrills. They have gone through a miracle, a dark age, a Hall of Fame coach and a chosen one, each run further solidifying their legacy. This book has shown that the Cavaliers have been one of the most successful and beloved NBA teams for the past forty years. With the young nucleus and passion of the loyal city behind them, it won't be long before the Cavs are back in the championship, this time holding gold when the final buzzer sounds!

By the Numbers

HEAD COACHES

Bill Fitch	1970–79	Mike Fratello	1993–99
Stan Albeck	1979–80	Randy Wittman	1999–2001
Bill Musselman	1980–81	John Lucas	2001–03
Don Delaney	1981	Keith Smart	2003
Bob Kloppenburg	1981	Paul Silas	2003–05
Chuck Daly	1981–82	Brendan Malone	2005
Bill Musselman	1982	Mike Brown	2005–10
Tom Nissalke	1982–84	Byron Scott	2010–13
George Karl	1984–86	Mike Brown	2013–2014
Gene Littles	1986	David Blatt	2014–Present
Lenny Wilkens	1986–93		

RETIRED JERSEYS

Jersey Number	Player	Position	Years with Cavs
7	Bobby "Bingo" Smith	G/F	1970–79
11	Zydrunas Ilgauskas	C	1997–2010
22	Larry Nance	F	1988–94
25	Mark Price	G	1986–95
34	Austin Carr	G	1971–80
42	Nate Thurmond	C	1975–77
43	Brad Daugherty	C	1986–94

FRANCHISE LEADERS

Games Started—Zydrunas Ilgauskas (673)
Minutes Played—LeBron James (22,105)
Field Goals Made—LeBron James (5,415)
Field Goal Attempts—LeBron James (11,403)
Three-Point Field Goals Made—Mark Price (802)
Three-Point Field Goal Attempts—LeBron James (2,244)
Free Throws Made—LeBron James (3,650)
Free Throw Attempts—LeBron James (4,917)
Offensive Rebounds—Zydrunas Ilgauskas (2,336)
Defensive Rebounds—Brad Daugherty (4,020)
Total Rebounds—Zydrunas Ilgauskas (5,904)
Assists—Mark Price (4,206)
Steals—LeBron James (955)
Blocked Shots—Zydrunas Ilgauskas (1,269)
Points—LeBron James (15,251)

Index

About the Author

Courtesy of www.vpeterpress.com.

Vince McKee is a growing force in the sports literary world and is rapidly becoming the go-to source on all things Cleveland sports. His first three books—*Hero*, *Cleveland's Finest* and *Jacobs Field*—exploded onto Amazon's bestseller list upon release. Vince is the lead writer for www.vpeterpress. com and currently travels the globe further spreading the message of *Hero*. He is always willing to speak with fans and critics and can be reached at coachvin14@ yahoo.com, or you can follow him on Twitter at VinceTheAuthor. Vince enjoys spending as much time as possible with his wife, Emily, and daughter, Maggie.

Visit us at
www.historypress.net
....
This title is also available as an e-book